GO INTO THE LAND!

The Great Commission from Joshua to Jesus

Dr. Joseph Davis

Copyright © 2025 by **Joseph Davis**

All rights reserved. No part of this publication may be reproduced, distributed, or transmitted in any form or by any means, without prior written permission.

Scripture quotations marked (ESV) are taken from the ESV® Bible (The Holy Bible, English Standard Version®), © 2001 by Crossway, a publishing ministry of Good News Publishers. Used by permission. All rights reserved.

Cover design by Jenneth Dyck.

Published by Mammoth Holler. Stuarts Draft, Virginia, U.S.A.

Go into the Land!: The Great Commission from Joshua to Jesus / Joseph Davis
ISBN-13: 978-1-960180-09-4

CONTENTS

Joshua and Jesus iii
Moses Is Dead (Joshua 1:1–9) 1
Unified Obedience (Joshua 1:10–18) 11
Stories About God (Joshua 2:1–14) 23
Rahab's First Passover (Joshua 2:15–24) 33
Miraculous Unity (Joshua 3) 45
Stones to Remember (Joshua 4) 55
A Fresh Start (Joshua 5:1–12) 67
Is God on Your Side (Joshua 5:13–15) 79
Six Days of Trumpets (Joshua 6:1–14) 87
Joy on Judgment Day (Joshua 6:15–27) 99
Achan's Sin: God's Correction (Joshua 7) 111
Achan's Sin: Revealing and Removing Evil (Joshua 7) 123
Ai Moments (Joshua 8:1–23) 135
Strangers at Mount Ebal (Joshua 8:24–35) 147
Grace for Gibeonites: Redeemed Despite Ourselves (Joshua 9) 159
Grace for Gibeonites: Who Can Stand Against Us? (Joshua 10:1–15) 171
Land Left to Conquer (Joshua 10:16–13:7) 183
Wasting an Inheritance (Joshua 13:8–19:51 & 21:1–42) 193

Running to Refuge (Joshua 20) 205
Keeping Promises (Joshua 21:43–22:9) 215
Protecting Unity (Joshua 22:10–34) 225
Teaching the Next Generation (Joshua 23) 237
A Monument for Renewal (Joshua 24:1–28) 249
A Legacy Inspiring Faithfulness (Joshua 24:29–33) 261
About the Author 273

PREFACE

Joshua and Jesus

Welcome to this journey through the book of Joshua, a narrative of courageous and obedient faith that transcends its ancient setting. This is the story of a man tasked by God with the monumental mission of leading Israel into the promised land after forty years of wandering in the desert. Joshua's leadership, and how God's people responded, have much to teach us about our Great Commission from Jesus.

Delving into the experiences of Joshua and the Israelites, we'll witness their encounters with fearsome enemies, daunting obstacles, hidden evil, and the corrective judgment of a loving God. We will discover, too, the ways He blessed their faith and unified obedience.

Sometimes, God's people falter and seem undeserving, yet He remains faithful to His promises. That includes His promise to be with us, strengthening us, as we venture into the places He commands us to go.

As we follow Joshua's story, I'll highlight key historical context, powerful theological truths, and personal applications for all of us who seek to follow Jesus. We'll see, too, how the book of Joshua foreshadows the Day of the Lord, and the conflicts between the church and the forces of evil, described in Revelation.

Let's embark on this journey together, uncovering the profound inspiration and encouragement that the book of Joshua has to offer us. And let's also prepare to go into the world for Jesus, bringing His truth and light, the way Joshua and the Israelites went into the promised land. In doing so, we'll help establish a legacy of faithfulness for the generations.

CHAPTER ONE

Moses Is Dead
(Joshua 1:1–9)

HISTORY—MOSES AND JOSHUA

This story starts in dramatic fashion as Moses, the man Joshua had looked up to his whole life, had died. Joshua 1:1–2 recounts:

> *After the death of Moses, the servant of the LORD, the LORD said to Joshua, the son of Nun, Moses' assistant,* ² *"Moses my servant is dead."*

Moses, revered by all for his courage and leadership, was the only leader two generations of Israelites had ever known. This was the man God used to send plagues on Egypt, part the Red Sea, bring water from rocks, and provide manna from heaven, a pillar of fire at night, and a cloud by day. He was the one God inspired to write the first five books of the Bible. God gave him the tablets with the Ten Commandments. Moses had been a titan of faith, an example to every Israelite. Suddenly, Moses was gone. It was an emotional transition, thrusting Joshua into the spotlight. He must now fill Moses' shoes.

But, before we delve into the heart of this story, it's crucial to set the stage. What led them to this moment? Rewind to two years after the Israelites escaped Egypt. Moses had led the entire nation of Israel to the very doorstep of the promised land. God instructed Moses to send twelve spies, one from each tribe, to scout the land so they could prepare for its conquest. When they returned, all twelve confirmed the land's incredible beauty and fertility, a place "that flows with milk and honey" (Numbers 14:8).

However, they also reported formidable, well-fortified cities with armies of towering giants so big they made the spies feel like grasshoppers. Believing the conquest of the promised land to be an impossible task, their faith faltered in the face of adversity. Never mind how they had all personally witnessed God's power during their exodus from Egypt only two years prior! They were there for the plagues, the parting of the Red Sea, the destruction of Pharaoh's army, all of it. But that was yesterday. When confronted with this new, intimidating challenge, ten of the twelve spies were overcome with fear.

Only two of the twelve, Caleb and Joshua, were immediately ready to go into the land and take it. Numbers 14:6–10 describes their report:

> *And Joshua the son of Nun and Caleb the son of Jephunneh, who were among those who had spied out the land, tore their clothes* [7] *and said to all the congregation of the people of Israel, "The land, which we passed through to spy it out, is an exceedingly good land.* [8] *If the LORD delights in us, he will bring us into this land and give it to us, a land that flows with milk and honey.* [9] *Only do not rebel against the LORD. And do not fear the people of the land, for they are bread for us. Their protection is removed from them, and the LORD is with us; do not fear them."* [10] *Then all the congregation said to stone them with stones. But the glory of the LORD appeared at the tent of meeting to all the people of Israel.*

Joshua and Caleb were unable to persuade the rest of the spies. As a result, the entire nation of Israel heeded the warnings of the ten and chose the safety of the desert instead of going into the land to claim their inheritance. For the next thirty-eight years, God allowed them to live with the consequences of choosing safety instead of victory and comfort instead of destiny. The desert was the safe option; victory and destiny born of faith were the dangerous option. For us, too, safety is sometimes more appealing than victory or destiny, especially if it requires faith or sacrifice.

Numbers 14:28–30 continues the story:

> *As I live, declares the LORD, what you have said in my hearing I will do to you:* [29] *your dead bodies shall fall in this wilderness, and of all your number, listed in the census from twenty years old and upward, who have*

> *grumbled against me, ³⁰ not one shall come into the land where I swore that I would make you dwell, except Caleb the son of Jephunneh and Joshua the son of Nun.*

For thirty-eight years, the fearful, faithless, grumbling generation lived out their lives in the desert a stone's throw from the promised land, as the next generation waited. During that period, God instructed Moses to name Joshua his successor. For nearly four decades, Moses mentored Joshua, preparing for the day he would lead God's people into the land.

THEOLOGY—IT'S YOUR TIME, JOSHUA

Joshua 1:3–9 recalls God's instructions to Joshua and the Israelites:

> *Now therefore arise, go over this Jordan, you and all this people, into the land I am giving to them, to the people of Israel. Every place that the sole of your foot will tread upon I have given to you, just as I promised to Moses. ⁴ From the wilderness and this Lebanon as far as the great river, the river Euphrates, all the land of the Hittites to the Great Sea toward the going down of the sun shall be your territory. ⁵ No man shall be able to stand before you all the days of your life. Just as I was with Moses, so I will be with you. I will not leave you or forsake you. ⁶ Be strong and courageous, for you shall cause this people to inherit the land that I swore to their fathers to give them. ⁷ Only be strong and very courageous, being careful to do according to all the law that Moses my servant commanded you. Do not turn*

from it to the right hand or to the left, [so] that you may have good success wherever you go. ⁸ This Book of the Law shall not depart from your mouth, but you shall meditate on it day and night, so that you may be careful to do according to all that is written in it. For then you will make your way prosperous, and then you will have good success. ⁹ Have I not commanded you? Be strong and courageous. Do not be frightened, and do not be dismayed, for the LORD your God is with you wherever you go."

Joshua was grieving. His friend and mentor had died, and now God had thrust him into leadership. Here's another way of phrasing the words God spoke to him:

"Joshua, the task your mentor Moses could not complete is now yours. You will lead My people into the promised land. You are going to shepherd and inspire these people who have, by their own choice, wandered aimlessly in fear for four decades. You will organize these rebellious nomads into a formidable invasion force. But it won't be easy. You will need strength and courage. There will be days of great victory when you'll feel like there's nothing you can't do. You'll be so proud of your people. There will also be days of crushing defeat when your people's actions will leave you so frustrated, you'll feel like quitting.

"So, you'll need to remember everything Moses taught you, both by his example and by the written words he has left behind. You'll need to remember everything I told Moses to write in Genesis, Exodus, Leviticus, Numbers, and Deuteronomy. You will turn to Genesis when you need to be reminded of My divine power in creation and redemption. You will learn from the lives of Adam and Eve, Cain and Abel, and Joseph. You will learn a lot about how to deal with my people from those stories. Remember the exodus from Egypt. Read and learn lessons from all of Moses' triumphs and failures in that book. Heed the commandments I set forth in Leviticus and the revised versions I gave this younger generation, your generation, in Deuteronomy. You have been tasked with a monumental undertaking, but through the words I have inspired Moses to write, you also carry with you the wisdom of the ages."

You Will Not Fail

Joshua 1:8 is an often-misunderstood scripture. Many perceive it as a conditional promise for earthly success. But this whole introductory passage, where God speaks to a grieving, anxious Joshua, isn't a command. Reread Joshua 1:8 as the promise it is:

> *This Book of the Law shall not depart from your mouth, but you shall meditate on it day and night, so that you may be careful to do according to all that is written in it. For then you will make your way prosperous, and then you will have good success.*

In other words, God said: "I know all five of those books are a lot to remember, Joshua, but here's the good news. You won't have to bear it alone. I will implant the teachings of Moses deep within your heart, keep them on your lips, and give you wisdom to understand them. By My spirit, I will help you recall each lesson and instruction exactly when you need it! I'll keep you on the right path. I won't let you waver to the left or right. This is why you will prosper and succeed. Because I have placed you at the very center of My divine, sovereign plan, your success is guaranteed, no matter what! You are about to embark on the path I have prepared for you way in advance." (See Ephesians 2:10 for more about the paths God lays for us ahead of time.)

"Listen, Joshua! Just as I was with Moses during the Exodus, I will be with you as you lead Israel into the promised land. Under your leadership, I will make My people into an unstoppable force. And in the darkest moments, remember, I will never leave you or forsake you. Through you, I will keep My promises to Israel."

PERSONAL—STRENGTH AND COURAGE

How can you be sure you'll always have enough strength and courage to obey all of God's commands, no matter what? In His instructions, reassurance, and promise to Joshua, we hear an echo of Jesus' great commission of His disciples in Matthew 28:18–20:

> *And Jesus came and said to them, "All authority in heaven and on earth has been given to me.* [19] *Go therefore and make disciples of all nations, baptizing them in the name of the Father and of the Son and of the Holy Spirit,* [20] *teaching them to observe all that I have*

commanded you. And behold, I am with you always, to the end of the age."

Just like in Joshua's battle, our opponent isn't mere flesh and blood; it's the forces of darkness and evil. The promises in Joshua and in Matthew 28 aren't about fleeting earthly prosperity. They are about Joshua's role, and our role, in an eternal kingdom. They emphasize the power of faith, obedience, and the promise of God's presence in fulfilling His divine plan. They both assure us that no matter what, God will *never* leave or forsake His chosen people!

What God has called us, like Joshua, to do will put us in exceedingly difficult situations. There will be many bad days. Sometimes, what we are called to do will be rejected by the vast majority; it won't be popular. Wouldn't it be great to be equipped with everything we need to stay strong and courageous in the face of such opposition? Wouldn't it be great to know how to spot God's presence no matter how terrible things are going? Well, according to Jesus, we're ready for those dark times.

Remember God's promise in Joshua 1:8. It isn't about earthly, political, personal, financial, or emotional success. It speaks of a righteous calling God has prepared beforehand, which we will walk into. This promise says that God, through His spirit, will write His commands on our hearts, equipping us with everything we need to succeed as we venture into our promised land with the gospel, to fulfill His great commission! Because of this promise, we will have the strength and courage to succeed in what God has called us to do.

We find similar encouragement in God's promise of His help and presence in Hebrews 13:5–6:

Keep your life free from love of money and be content with what you have, for he has said, "I will never leave you nor forsake you." [6] *So we can confidently say, "The Lord is my helper; I will not fear; what can man do to me?"*

I see the command to "go into the land" as a metaphor for stepping out courageously in faith and obedience to God's command in the Great Commission. Like Joshua, we are commanded to go into the land. But, we aren't entering a place to conquer it militarily, culturally, or politically. Instead, we are commanded to go forward and make disciples of all nations, baptizing and teaching them everything Jesus has taught us. That's why the prosperity and success God promises us when we go into the land isn't earthly success: our true destiny is our victorious role in God's unstoppable plan of redemption!

While God does call us to these things, stepping up to fulfill God's calling can be scary at times. Why else would He tell us to be strong and courageous? After all, you wouldn't need reminders about strength and courage if you weren't doing anything important. Hearing a call to serve can be exciting, but it can also be daunting. God knows our inclination is to be fearful, guarded, and paralyzed. Trust me, we've all been there.

It's natural to be fearful and uncertain. No doubt, we all need courage because the forces of evil want us, like Israel, to be so full of fear we never even start. For us to be successful in what we've been called to do, we too will have to put our trust in the promise God made to Joshua: He will never leave, forsake, or fail to provide for us as we enter uncharted territory for His kingdom.

You might be afraid of what God is calling you to do, with all its obstacles, uncertainties, and unforeseen challenges. What Kingdom tasks are you afraid to undertake? Which ones seem impossible because of your own earthly fears? Have you chosen to stay on the other side of the Jordan, wandering without strength and courage, in the illusion of a safe desert?

It's true, there are days when you're just not going to be strong. There are days when you won't have enough courage, though everything within you wants to be strong and courageous. Yet, you don't need to live like the depressed, frightened, grumbling generation that wandered for forty years until they died. You don't need to be afraid to undertake great things for God's kingdom or to do what He has commanded. God has called us, and He's promised never to leave us or forsake us.

Why would you want to live in the desert another day, let alone another year? Life's not that great on this side of the Jordan, if you haven't noticed. It's a desert! We're all a little scared, but it's time to have strength and courage, cross the river, and go into the land!

CHAPTER TWO

Unified Obedience
(Joshua 1:10–18)

As a follower of Jesus, what do you believe obedience will look like, going into the land with the gospel? Maybe you'll stop cussing so much? Maybe you'll become more faithful in your giving or in church attendance? Or, perhaps obedience is defined by personal integrity or morality? Certainly, some of those things can be a part of your obedience. They are all, in fact, different types of individual obedience.

This may surprise you, but individual obedience, while important, isn't the most important aspect of our obedience. God has called us to something much more important: unified community obedience. As we go into the land, God's people will never prosper if we're only individuals working diligently to adhere to personal biblical standards. A church made up of people focused solely on individual obedience resembles a man-made religion. By itself, there's no real power in that. God's people cannot thrive together when individual obedience is our primary focus.

What if I told you that successful obedience to God's call depends just as much on the people around you as it does on your own efforts? What if I told you the only way to be truly obedient is in community?

In Joshua 1:10–18, Joshua issued orders, and the Israelites committed to follow his instructions faithfully in strength and courage:

> *Joshua commanded the officers of the people, ⁱⁱ "Pass through the midst of the camp and command the people, 'Prepare your provisions; for within three days you are to pass over this Jordan, to go in to take possession of the land that the LORD your God is giving you to possess.'" ¹² And to the Reubenites, the Gadites, and the half-tribe of Manasseh, Joshua said, ¹³ "Remember the word that Moses the servant of the LORD commanded you, saying, 'The LORD your God is providing you a place of rest and will give you this land.' ¹⁴ Your wives, your little ones, and your livestock shall remain in the land that Moses gave you beyond the Jordan, but all the men of valor among you shall pass over armed before your brothers and shall help them, ¹⁵ until the LORD gives rest to your brothers as he has to you, and they also take possession of the land that the LORD your God is giving them. Then you shall return to the land of your possession and shall possess it, the land that Moses the servant of the LORD gave you beyond the Jordan*

toward the sunrise." ¹⁶ *And they answered Joshua, "All that you have commanded us we will do, and wherever you send us we will go.* ¹⁷ *Just as we obeyed Moses in all things, so we will obey you. Only be strong and courageous.* ¹⁸ *Whoever rebels against your commandment and disobeys your words, whatever you command him, shall be put to death. Only be strong and courageous."*

History—Pack Up

Three Days' Notice

Joshua had just been given a monumental task, along with a command to be strong and courageous. He took immediate action. He quickly gathered the leaders of every tribe and told them, "It's time; you have three days to prepare. Gather your tents, your sheep, your kids, your wives, your dogs, your clothes—everything. We are leaving this desert. The entire nation will cross this river into our new home. It's time to go into the land God has commanded us to enter." Notice, there was no debate, negotiation, or complaining, which were the habits of the previous, faithless generation who chose comfort over promise. The new generation of Israelites weren't waiting for the spies to come back with their report. There were no battle plans or strategies. They just started packing. They were all in, together, unified in their obedience to what God had commanded!

Promise Keepers

Then Joshua went to the leaders of the tribes of Reuben and Gad, and the half-tribe of Manasseh, who were primarily cattle herders. They had made a previous deal with Moses to stay on the other side of Jordan because those plains were perfect for cattle. In Numbers 32:16–17, they had committed to their common purpose with the rest of the Israelites:

> *We will build sheepfolds here for our livestock and cities for our little ones, [17] but we will take up arms, ready to go before the people of Israel until we have brought them to their place.*

So, those tribes received their inheritance early from Moses, but only with a promise they would join the rest of Israel in battle when the time came. Now Moses was dead, and that time had come. Joshua appealed to them to honor their covenant with Moses. They already had everything needed for prosperity: land, cities, families, livelihoods. Their life plans were set. They could have made various excuses, like, "We already conquered our land. Why risk everything for land we won't even live in?" Or "Our deal was with Moses, and he's dead. We're not obligated to you, Joshua; we didn't make any promises to you."

But, that wasn't their response at all. They didn't hesitate or say, "Let us think about it." They didn't go back on their word. Leaving half the men to protect their families, they sent their finest warriors with Joshua across the Jordan. Out of love for their brethren, they honored their promise to Moses without delay or conditions. They were loyal to God and to their fellow Israelites. While Israel may have been twelve different tribes, for that moment they were all inspired to trust, act, and obey God together, as one unified people.

Theology—Unified in Faith

Immediate Obedience

On that day, God's promise to Abraham four hundred years prior finally materialized. It was a powerful moment, and all the people were humbled by God's amazing mercy and faithfulness. Under Joshua's guidance, the entire nation now embraced one unified focus: prepare to enter the land together, in community. They had their goal, they had a deadline, and they had the instructions they needed for that day. They were packing up to head out. Together, they eagerly anticipated this transition to a life of obedience to God's call.

Unlike the previous generation of worriers and complainers, they were collectively strong, courageous, faithful, and focused. They didn't postpone their obedience; they weren't afraid of unknowns or unanswered questions. They didn't have all the details, only the knowledge that they had three days to pack up everything and cross the Jordan into the promised land.

Once they crossed the Jordan, they would be past the point of no return. The river cut off any escape if a battle went badly. But, they had each other and their trust in the

Lord. They were united in faith that when the time arrived, God would reveal the next steps. And for today, they were going full speed ahead as one people.

Selfless Obedience

Let's consider once again the faithful obedience of those other two and a half tribes. They already had everything they needed for a prosperous earthly existence. Their life was good—successful, comfortable, and secure among their families—yet they were prepared to go into the land with the rest of the tribes! By being obedient, they risk everything.

Humanly speaking, this unified act of obedience by Joshua and Israel could be perceived as risky, irrational, even foolish. They didn't know what they were up against, and there would be no back-up plan, with their lives and families and possessions on the line. But, they shared the faith necessary to be fully reliant upon God for success, an entire nation unified in what looked from the outside like irrational obedience against their self-interest. This immediate, unified obedience was previously unthinkable. The only other time the Israelites as a nation had ever been joined in purpose to this degree was when they were unified in complaining. Where did their miraculous, unified faith and obedience come from? Paul's words in Philippians 2:13 give us insight:

> *For it is God who works in you, both to will and to work for his good pleasure.*

It was, in fact, the gift of faith the Spirit of God gave to the Israelites that produced their unity and obedience. The gift of faith inspired them to take extraordinary action as a community. They all stepped into what God had called them to. The gift of faith inspired them to set aside any personal agendas for the sake of their greater calling. Their prompt, unified, selfless obedience enabled them to experience tremendous unity, power, and love for one another! Full of strength and courage, they began a new way of life. Together, they were living by faith and not by sight. It was the same gift of faith from the Spirit of God, working in their hearts and stirring them to immediate obedience, that Jesus has given to us, His church!

PERSONAL—OBEDIENCE REQUIRES ALL OF US

Following Jesus requires immediate, unified obedience from all of God's people, *including you*. This miraculous, instant, faith-driven, communal obedience is most definitely something we should aspire to. Wouldn't it be great if believers everywhere—humbled and full of awe at God's faithfulness—came together with this type of obedient unity?

When Jesus commanded us to go into the land and make disciples of all nations, we were called to the same immediate, unified obedience as the Israelites. Paul explained in Galatians 3:29:

And if you are Christ's, then you are Abraham's offspring, heirs according to promise.

A similar promise of inheritance, coupled with the promise of God's help and presence (see Chapter One), inspired the Israelites' immediate, unified obedience. But, the gospel iteration of God's fulfilled promise is far greater than just taking the land of Canaan. Through Christ, we will inherit the earth!

However, this faithful, community obedience doesn't always come with all the answers ahead of time. True, unified obedience to our calling is filled with the unknown and earthly risk, as it was for the Israelites. It's natural to come up with excuses to delay obedience, to try to account for every scenario and manage the risk of Kingdom work. But, our delayed obedience isn't obedience. It's disobedience; it's us choosing our plans over God's plan.

In Philippians 2:2-4, Paul called God's people to look outside themselves, to each other and to unity in His purposes:

> *... complete my joy by being of the same mind, having the same love, being in full accord and of one mind. ³ Do nothing from selfish ambition or conceit, but in humility count others more significant than yourselves. ⁴ Let each of you look not only to his own interests but also to the interests of others.*

The church today, every one of us, has been called to this same type of immediate, unified obedience, in humility and love. We, too, are commanded to trust God's divine timing and provision, even when it contradicts our human wisdom.

God may be calling you to cross the river to a new way of life, in full-time Kingdom service. Like the new generation of Israelites in the desert, you're ready to live by faith, not by sight Today, you are being called to step out in faith, to trust God to provide for your needs and to provide a pathway. I had a call like that forty years ago, and it burned deep. I became restless; I couldn't envision doing anything else. It became my single driving focus, and everything else seemed like an obstacle. Your call to unified obedience might not feel exactly like that, yet it's still a passion and runs just as deep!

You may feel an intense urge to support, encourage, and uplift those stepping out in faith into the unknown. You're like the tribes who had already settled yet lovingly, joyfully desired to do anything they could to stand alongside the others.

Whether you are among those called to full-time service or among those called to support them faithfully, it's our shared duty to trust God's promises and obey His call. Our obedience can't be done alone: it must be in community! This isn't a mere aspiration. It isn't a call for a year down the line, once we have every detail or contingency sorted. It's a challenge for right now, today, no matter where we are in our journey—and it requires the gift of faith.

Paul emphasized the unifying nature of God's call on our lives, in Ephesians 4:1–4:

> *I ... urge you to walk in a manner worthy of the calling to which you have been called, ² with all humility and gentleness, with patience, bearing with one another in love, ³ eager to maintain the unity of the Spirit in the bond of peace. ⁴ There is one body and one Spirit—just as you were called to the one hope that belongs to your call.*

God may be calling you, like those twelve tribes, to a moment of preparation. No doubt, God still stirs His people and calls them to powerful moments of unified obedience, just like the Israelites' crossing of the river. Does it feel like you may be on the banks of the Jordan? Your next few steps will require that you live by faith.

That can be scary! There are so many unknowns. Have you planned well enough? Do you know the details? Will you have enough resources? Do you have enough help? Will you have enough supplies and enough money? No matter how well you plan, you cannot know for sure.

Without some risk and stepping out in faith, we will always have reasons to delay our unified obedience. For us to have the necessary courage, through faith, we will need to tap into this power of unified community. As the church, we've been sitting on the banks of our Jordan long enough. Have you started packing? Are others around you packing while you sit comfortably? The time to move is now.

For those who are ready to cross the Jordan into a new life of service to God, it's going to require a lot of faith and trust. For those ready to heed the call to extend your hand and walk alongside one other, you will need the same faith and trust. If we're going to live by faith, it can only happen within a community committed to unified and immediate obedience. That's the only way we will have sufficient strength and courage, especially when the details of our path remain unclear. We need each other.

CHAPTER THREE

Stories About God
(Joshua 2:1–14)

Have you ever heard what some might call a "God story"? A story about how God intervened in someone's life? Perhaps it was a story of God orchestrating extraordinary circumstances, preserving someone's life against all odds. Maybe it was a story of transformation where someone hostile to the gospel unexpectedly began to follow Jesus. Maybe it was a story about someone who remained faithful to Jesus despite incredible persecution or pressure. Maybe it was a story about how, through God's mercy, someone overcame earthly obstacles or challenges in a surprising way.

Psalm 105:1–2 calls on God's people to tell stories about Him to glorify Him:

> *Oh give thanks to the LORD; call upon his name; make known his deeds among the peoples! ² Sing to him, sing praises to him; tell of all his wondrous works!*

These powerful, inspiring, engaging God stories are one of the things that makes the church so effective. Hearing or witnessing many of these deeply cherished stories firsthand is a privilege. As you learn the details of so many people's God stories over time, your faith will be strengthened by them, as mine has.

This chapter has two goals: First, to help you see the power in your own redemption story and to tell it more often. Second, to inspire you to discover the stories of your brothers and sisters, and to celebrate and proclaim those narratives, too.

In Joshua 2:1 and 2:8–11, two of Joshua's spies snuck into Jericho, where a local woman named Rahab recalled in awe the Israelites' powerful God story:

> *And Joshua the son of Nun sent two men secretly from Shittim as spies, saying, "Go, view the land, especially Jericho." They went and came into the house of a prostitute named Rahab and lodged there. . . . ⁸ Before the men lay down, she came up to them on the roof ⁹ and said to the men, "I know that the LORD has given you the land, and that the fear of you has fallen upon us, and that all the inhabitants of the land melt away before you. ¹⁰ For we have heard how the LORD dried up the water of the Red Sea before you when you came out of Egypt, and what you did to the two kings of the Amorites who were beyond the Jordan, to Sihon and Og,*

whom you devoted to destruction. ¹¹ And as soon as we heard it, our hearts melted, and there was no spirit left in any man because of you, for the LORD *your God, he is God in the heavens above and on the earth beneath.*

HISTORY—HOW NEWS TRAVELED

In the ancient world, significant news spread primarily through individuals traveling from one region to another. Travelers, traders, spies, scouts, and messengers relayed firsthand or secondhand accounts. The more extraordinary the news, the greater the degree of skepticism people maintained until the story could be verified further. Verification started with the number of people carrying the news and the uniformity of their accounts. For something to be considered more than a tall tale or rumor, it required a multitude of different reporters. This was likely how the people living in Canaan learned of three of the greatest military upsets in history.

The remarkable news that Pharaoh's army was drowned at the Red Sea and that two formidable Amorite kings were defeated by a nation of nomadic former slaves would have qualified as extraordinary events needing witnesses to verify. After Pharaoh released Israel from slavery, he changed his mind and decided to pursue them with his powerful army. The Israelites were trapped between the sea and the Egyptian army until God parted the Red Sea, which allowed the former slaves to escape. Once the last Israelite crossed to the other shore, the sea closed, and the deluge drowned Pharaoh's army. This story would have terrified other nations. When people in Canaan heard about all God had done for Israel, they probably sent scouts to see for themselves. Trusted scouts and spies would have reported back to their kings the firsthand verification they obtained—or if the story wasn't true, they would expose it as a fraud.

Nearly forty years later, the Israelites were near the edge of the promised land, seeking peaceful passage through Amorite territories. Two renowned Amorite kings, Sihon and Og, refused to give permission and instead sent their armies to destroy Israel. But God promised Israel they would rout both kings in two separate battles, and that's exactly what happened. News of these stunning, verifiable victories, combined with the Red Sea event forty years earlier, would have troubled nearby nations. Israel now had a reputation of formidable military power, courtesy of their God, and the word was spreading.

Rahab testified that the people of Jericho knew of these God stories, as well as the claims that He was going to give their land to His people, the Israelites. Jericho sent its own spies. They saw the Israelites packing up and preparing to cross the Jordan; they were coming soon. The hearts of the people of Jericho had "melted with fear." Meanwhile, Jericho had also been tracking Joshua's spies, who were now in serious danger.

Theology—"What God Has Done"

Stories of God's Sovereignty

The incredible stories of the Israelites' victories were made believable by God strategically using a multitude of credible traveling witnesses. His plan of redemption has always included the proclamation of stories about His mighty works, declared to people in all the nations. Those stories, and the people who hear, proclaim, and are transformed by them, are all part of God's sovereign plan.

This story of Rahab, a marginalized woman with no status or important connections in society, shows just how powerful these stories were. The accounts of what God did at the Red Sea and in the battles with the Amorites are stories God used to save her! It might seem strange for the Israelite spies to turn to a "random" Canaanite prostitute for help. How did they find her? What were they doing in her house? The spies had never even been to Jericho before. There's no way they knew her beforehand. This aspect of the story is itself an incredible example of God revealing how He works all things together for His plan of redemption for His people. Isn't it awesome when God fulfills His plan through the most unexpected people in the most unlikely places?

When God saves you, He doesn't care about your past, because through Christ, He is rewriting your story. God prepared Rahab for this good work beforehand, and because He gave her faith, she tripped and fell right into His plan. Rahab's faith set her apart. Unlike those who were frightened by these stories of God's mighty works, she put her trust in them. History, combined with faith, gave her the wisdom and courage to abandon a way of life that had existed for hundreds of years. By faith, when she heard these stories, she was able to see that the only rational response was to live by faith and not by sight. By faith, she knew Jericho, which appears to be an undefeatable fortress town, would be no match for the power of God. By faith, she took bold action an unbeliever would never consider. Her faith inspired her courageous, decisive obedience. All she wanted was to be among the people of God—to be a part of His covenant with Abraham.

Stories of Promises Kept

Rahab's story can be seen as a beautiful metaphor for all unlikely people, throughout every age, who are fully accepted into God's covenant by faith. Rahab was a Gentile (non-Hebrew) prostitute, the last person the Israelites would expect to be an example of faithfulness. But God made Rahab an heir to all the promises He made to Abraham, including His promise to bring people from all nations into His covenant with His people. And then, there's the promise made to her entire family. They, too, become part of God's covenant relationship with His people!

How did this all happen? By God's grace, Rahab heard the stories about mighty things God had done for the Israelites. In fact, Rahab's redemption story became just as important as the story of the Red Sea, or of those battles won in the wilderness. Why else would this otherwise unknown woman be mentioned in other places in Scripture, including the New Testament? This was how the story of God's covenant with Abraham was spread, how Abraham became a blessing to all nations. This is also how the gospel, which fulfills and replaces God's covenant with Abraham, becomes the message we carry.

PERSONAL—WE HAVE STORIES TO TELL

One of the most powerful tools the church has is the personal stories of miracles God has done through the gospel. The stories of what God did for Israel stirred Rahab's heart, preparing her for a life-changing encounter. He also uses our personal God stories to prepare the hearts of those around us for the return of Jesus Christ, because there is power in firsthand, eyewitness testimony to what God is doing in the hearts of His people.

I remember a story of another marginalized woman in the New Testament whom God used to save many unlikely people. John 4:28–39 recalls how a woman in Samaria, a Gentile-influenced country on the margins of Judea, spread the God story of her encounter with Jesus at the town well:

> *So the woman left her water jar and went away into town and said to the people, "Come, see a man who told me all that I ever did. Can this be the Christ?" ...*
> *39 Many Samaritans from that town believed in him*

> *because of the woman's testimony, "He told me all that I ever did."*

The New Testament is full of other amazing transformation stories, like Paul's conversion, described in Acts 9:21–22:

> *All who heard him were amazed and said, "Is not this the man who made havoc in Jerusalem of those who called upon this name?...* [22] *But Saul increased all the more in strength, and confounded the Jews who lived in Damascus by proving that Jesus was the Christ.*

A story of redemption, every last one, is powerful good news about what God has done. When people hear these stories, some will reject them, ignore them, scoff at them, or be angry at you for sharing them. But, there will be others, like Rahab and the woman at the well, whom God has prepared to hear and follow the Lamb. Proclaiming the gospel isn't just some theological overview about the cross or justification by faith. The gospel was always intended to include stories of what Jesus has done in the hearts and lives of His chosen people. God loves to use stories about His amazing goodness, His faithfulness, and the miraculous transformation He has effected in our lives. He loves it when we spread those stories to those who have ears to hear them—it makes Him smile every time! God also uses these stories to strengthen us when we get distracted or discouraged. This is why it's important to share the great things God has done in the hearts of many believers.

The multitude of redemption stories is undeniable verification, and an encouraging reminder, of God's love and grace. There is nothing any skeptic, atheist, or anyone else can say to refute verified, miraculous stories of redemption, restoration, and transformation. Psalm 96:2–3 echoes the Great Commission with its call to tell stories "among the nations" of His glory and the salvation He brings:

> *Sing to the Lord, bless his name; tell of his salvation from day to day. ³ Declare his glory among the nations, his marvelous works among all the peoples!"*

I've had lunches with other pastors in which we spent an hour just swapping the redemption stories from our congregations. I am amazed by what God has done in the lives of people I know in my own church, the stories of how God brought them through pain, tragedy, and transformation, and how He is using them in the lives of others. The most unlikely people have been made into the best church family I've ever been part of. I know your local church is also full of powerful personal stories of redemption! We should take the time to learn them, celebrate them, and tell others about them.

If we're going to spread the good news of our redemption stories to marginalized people—which is who we all were before Jesus—we *must* talk about the mighty works of God in our lives. As we venture into the land we have been promised, we should declare what God has done for us and what He has done for others in our churches. They are more than stories of how God saved us; they are stories that prove God redeems and keeps His promises! Our stories and those of our brothers and sisters carry hope and encouragement as God uses them to call new people to follow Jesus and strengthen us when we need it most.

Do you see your own story as part of God's grand gospel redemption narrative? You should! Because every follower of Jesus has a God story worthy to be proclaimed, which can inspire and encourage others. Let's not hesitate to share them.

CHAPTER FOUR

Rahab's First Passover
(Joshua 2:15–24)

Do you ever forget important things? Locking a door, or bringing your cell or wallet, when you leave the house? Birthdays—or heaven forbid, men, your anniversary?

Have you heard stories about someone leaving a critical component out of a repair or an assembly? Have you ever been given an important task where you forgot a critical part that resulted in failure or starting over? Forgetting can have a range of consequences, from annoying to frustrating, expensive, or even catastrophic.

If you think about it, remembering important stuff is a huge part of life we must put a lot of effort into. To make sure we remember important things, we write lists, use digital tools and visual aids, and develop routines. We use holidays to remember important milestones, people, and historic events, even the tragic ones. We keep precious things that don't mean much to others but keep our memories fresh about loved ones no longer with us. The more precious or critical remembering becomes, the more careful we become to make sure we never forget.

As the church following the Lamb into the land, the most important thing we need to remember is *why* we go into the land. That may seem obvious, but going into the land is complicated. There are distractions, challenges, hardships, and suffering. We need constant reminders about the important things in our mission: the why, the how, the what, and the who.

HISTORY—A PERFECT ESCAPE PLAN

The Perfect House

Joshua 2:15–16 recounts how Rahab helped the Israelite spies escape Jericho:

> *Then she let them down by a rope through the window, for her house was built into the city wall, so that she lived in the wall. ¹⁶ And she said to them, "Go into the hills, or the pursuers will encounter you, and hide there three days until the pursuers have returned. Then afterward you may go your way."*

Rahab lived in perhaps the least appealing location, built into the fortified walls of an ancient city. Its long distance from the amenities at the city center, its vulnerability to invasions, and its proximity to the dumping spots for waste and sewage weren't exactly selling points. Her house likely had one entrance, an elevated window, making access inconvenient and uncomfortable.

The house symbolized Rahab's social marginalization as a single woman and a prostitute. She was culturally, spiritually, and residentially on the fringes of Jericho. I wonder if her marginalization helped her see the hopelessness of Jericho's situation and convinced her to hope in God instead. The location and layout of her house are some of the more fascinating, yet largely ignored, details of her incredible story. By God's sovereign plan, she was uniquely situated to provide the exact things Joshua's spies need to escape the city. I love how God planned every detail, right down to her house in the city wall, to position Rahab for faithful obedience.

Rahab hid the spies and tricked the spy hunters: "Hurry! Chase them! Maybe you'll catch them on their way to the Jordan!" (See Joshua 2:4–7.) These spy police fell for her misdirection. They left the city near nightfall, and the city gate closed behind them as they departed. (Why the would-be spy catchers, given the critical nature of their job, took the advice of a prostitute living in the wall is a bit bewildering.) At night, with the city gates closed, Rahab lowered the spies through her window, which opened to the outside of Jericho's walls.

The Scarlet Rope

In Joshua 2:17–21, the spies made a promise to save Rahab and her family when the Israelite army descended on Jericho:

> *The men said to her, "We will be guiltless with respect to this oath of yours that you have made us swear. ^{18} Behold, when we come into the land, you shall tie this scarlet cord in the window through which you let us down, and you shall gather into your house your father and mother, your brothers, and all your father's household. ^{19} Then if anyone goes out of the doors of your house into the street, his blood shall be on his own head, and we shall be guiltless. But if a hand is laid on anyone who is with you in the house, his blood shall be on our head. ^{20} But if you tell this business of ours, then we shall be guiltless with respect to your oath that you have made us swear." ^{21} And she said, "According to your words, so be it." Then she sent them away, and they departed. And she tied the scarlet cord in the window.*

As Joshua's spies left, they gave Rahab those specific instructions to follow to ensure her family's safety during the siege. They gave her a scarlet rope to hang from the window as a sign to the army of the Lord to spare everyone in that house. They warned her, "Stay inside together as a family until the battle is done. If anyone doesn't stick to the plan, their fate is on them, not us!" As we'll discover, Rahab shared these instructions with her family, who followed them perfectly so that all were saved.

A Good Report

Joshua 2:22–24 recalls the spies' escape from Jericho and return to Joshua:

> *They departed and went into the hills and remained there three days until the pursuers returned, and the pursuers searched all along the way and found nothing. ^{23} Then the two men returned. They came down from the hills and passed over and came to Joshua the son of Nun, and they told him all that had happened to them.*
>
> *^{24} And they said to Joshua, "Truly the LORD has given all the land into our hands. And also, all the inhabitants of the land melt away because of us."*

The spy hunters searched in the wrong direction the whole time and gave up, heading home empty-handed. This provided the perfect opportunity for Joshua's spies to return to their camp near the Jordan River undetected. They came back with a beautiful story of Rahab and God's intervention on their behalf—and an exciting report about Jericho's vulnerability. "The people of Jericho are full of fear! Let's go right now!" But, the siege would have to wait a couple more days.

THEOLOGY—A PASSOVER TO REMEMBER

Let's talk about the instructions to Rahab to tie the scarlet robe over her window, likely the same window of escape for the spies. Where would the spies have gotten this idea of putting something red over an opening and staying inside for protection? It's remarkably similar to the instructions God gave Israel in Egypt so they would be protected from the angel of death. Those directions are found in Exodus 12:22–24:

> Take a bunch of hyssop, dip it in the blood in the basin and touch the lintel and the two doorposts with the blood in the basin. None of you shall go out of the door of his house until the morning. ²³ For the LORD will pass through to strike the Egyptians, and when he sees the blood on the lintel and on the two doorposts, the LORD will pass over the door and will not allow the destroyer to enter your houses to strike you. ²⁴ You shall observe this rite as a statute for you and for your sons forever.

Okay, you get one guess what time of year the siege of Jericho took place. Any takers? See Joshua 5:10 for the answer:

> While the people of Israel were encamped at Gilgal, they kept the Passover on the fourteenth day of the month in the evening on the plains of Jericho.

The day after the first Passover in the promised land, the siege on Jericho began—and if you think that's a coincidence, think again. All of this was by design. Joshua had a specific timetable for Jericho. He knew the calendar. After all, he remembered the very first Passover. The spies knew Joshua's timetable, too. It's not hard to believe the impending Passover inspired their idea.

Imagine the spies hiding under Rahab's thatched roof until nightfall, discussing this plan to spare Rahab and her family:

"Remember how God told us to put the blood over the doorposts so we'd be spared when He judged Egypt?"

"Yeah. Now that we are God's instrument of judgment on Jericho, let's give Raha the same kind of sign!"

"What if we told Rahab to use this scarlet rope and give her the same instructions God gave us in Egypt?"

"How cool would that be! We'll all see the scarlet rope in her window. Our brothers will be so fired up!"

"Exactly. They will remember what God did for us in Egypt and then see how God is doing the same thing for Rahab now."

Their instructions to Rahab were more than just some random plan. The scarlet hope would become a symbol of God's faithfulness. Rahab's hope was that the Passover symbol hanging in her window would remind Israel to pass over her house during the siege. And it worked, as we learn in Joshua 6:25:

> *But Rahab the prostitute and her father's household and all who belonged to her, Joshua saved alive. And she has lived in Israel to this day because she hid the messengers whom Joshua sent to spy out Jericho.*

The scarlet rope became another covenant sign, like Noah's rainbow, Abraham's circumcision, and our Lord's Supper. For Rahab, it would become a powerful reminder to her and her family about what God did for them personally. After forty Passovers—one in Egypt, thirty-nine in the wilderness—this was the best since the original, and it was Rahab's first! Every year after this one, Rahab probably celebrated two Passovers, Israel's and her personal Passover. For her, the scarlet rope, like blood over the door, would remind her of God's promise of protection from judgment.

For us, both Rahab's scarlet rope and the blood over the Israelites' doors remind us of the price of redemption: the blood of the Lamb of God. The fact that Rahab was a Gentile reminds us God's plan for redemption is for all His people, in any and every nation. It also shows how, while the first Passover was a memorable event, it foreshadowed the greatest Passover yet to come. That's the one in Revelation, the day all wickedness is judged and those covered by the blood of the Lamb will be saved. Aren't you glad God spared Israel in the first Passover in Egypt, Rahab in the fortieth Passover in Jericho, and you today?

Personal—Your Passover

The faithful obedience of Rahab, the Gentile prostitute, became renowned in Jewish history. Hebrews 11:31 records her entry in the "Hall of Faith":

> *By faith Rahab the prostitute did not perish with those who were disobedient, because she had given a friendly welcome to the spies.*

Read all of Hebrews 11 and see the luminaries of faith she's listed alongside: Abel, Enoch, Noah, Abraham, Sarah, Isaac, Jacob, Joseph, Moses and his parents, and the entire nation of Israel when they passed through the Red Sea on dry land. She is counted fully as one of God's people. In fact, God made Christ her direct descendant! (See Matthew 1:5.) That's right: Jesus was related to a Gentile prostitute. God's plans for the least likely of His people are more amazing than anything we could imagine!

Over the years, what do you think that scarlet rope meant to Rahab? Do you think she kept it? I bet she cherished it! I wonder if, after the battle, she kept it hanging in her window. Why would she want to take it down? It was a reminder of the covenant she made with the spies that day, how they remembered to spare her family. For Rahab, the scarlet rope became a reminder of the day faith aligned her with God, His plan, and His people. It reminded her of her first Passover, when God spared her from judgment just as He'd spared Israel forty years earlier. I don't know how much Rahab knew about Passover at first, but living with the Israelites over the years to follow, I'm sure she learned quite a bit. I wonder if her scarlet rope became part of their family tradition whenever her family celebrated Passover. Maybe they hung it in the window each year to remind them of their own personal

Passover story. And maybe, whenever the spies saw that rope in her window, it was a precious reminder for them, too.

Your Scarlet Rope

As Rahab's salvation was entirely dependent on a scarlet rope, so is ours, and His name is Jesus. In Romans 3:25, Paul explained how Jesus is our Passover Lamb, whose blood atoned for our sins—

> *[Christ Jesus,] whom God put forward as a propitiation by his blood, to be received by faith. This was to show God's righteousness, because in his divine forbearance he had passed over former sins.*

If you are a follower of Jesus, you too have your own personal Passover experience to remember. We all have our own scarlet rope we need to remember and cherish. It's Jesus—the cross, His blood, His promises. It's good to have reminders of what Christ has done. Yes, remembering Jesus seems obvious, but we forget every day. We have to make a point of reminding ourselves that no matter our past, we're not beyond the reach of God's sovereign grace and promises any more than Rahab was.

Our Jesus shed His blood on the cross once for all time as a sacrifice for your sins. Remember that your righteousness is not your own; you've been made righteous through Christ on the cross. Remember that because of Christ's blood, God sees you as one of His own, sealed you for salvation through faith. You, like Rahab, have been called out of Jericho to live among God's people as children of the promise! Remember to stand strong and courageous on those promises, even when everything around you is crumbling.

Recollect the promise Jesus made when He told us to go into the land He has given us power to overcome. He has promised, as we go into the land, to be with us until the land is ours at the end of the age. You will desperately need His presence, guidance, and protection every step of the way, because following the Lamb into the land, sharing everything Jesus taught us, will not be easy for you. As you go into the land, find ways to remember all the promises Jesus has made to you. You also must remember the cost of those promises, His blood shed for you on the cross. As you recall these things, may they inspire the kind of faithful obedience Rahab displayed regardless of danger. You can be strong and courageous just like Rahab was.

Go into the Land!

CHAPTER FIVE

Miraculous Unity
(Joshua 3)

Unity is a powerful idea. Most acknowledge that when people are unified, greater things can be accomplished. Have you ever experienced the joy of unity with a group of people? It's beautiful but, sadly, can rarely be sustained.

I remember how America was unified after 9/11. It was powerful. Everyone was unified, proud to be Americans. People were searching for answers; many turned to God. Churches, especially in New York City, were packed. America felt different. Then, about three months later, it was gone. That's how unity goes in this world. But, God's people cannot afford that fickle kind of unity. When it comes to following Jesus, our unity is mission critical.

Jesus and His apostles instructed us to pursue and preserve unity because going into the land would require it. How can we make sure the churches maintain their unity so we are all going in the same direction? What might cause us to become disunified? The answers to these questions are found in Joshua 3 and the account of the Israelites crossing the Jordan together. Joshua 3:1–5 begins the story:

> *Then Joshua rose early in the morning and they set out from Shittim. They came to the Jordan and lodged there before they passed over. ² At the end of three days, the officers went through the camp ³ and commanded the people, "As soon as you see the ark of the covenant of the* LORD *your God being carried by the Levitical priests, you shall set out from your place and follow it. ⁴ Yet there shall be a distance between you and it, about 2,000 cubits in length; do not come near it, [so] that you may know the way you shall go, for you have not passed this way before." ⁵ Then Joshua said to the people, "Consecrate yourselves, for tomorrow the* LORD *will do wonders among you."*

HISTORY—CROSSING THE JORDAN

The spies returned from Jericho with an incredible story about Rahab's faithfulness and the city's vulnerable state. With four days until Passover, everyone woke up early to begin the three-day journey to cross the Jordan River. This was a journey to a place they'd never been. They didn't know the land, the way, or the obstacles waiting for them. God told

Joshua, in effect, "I will show the people that I am with you and them in the same way I was with Moses and their parents."

This inspired Joshua. He gathered all the people and said, "Get ready, God will do some amazing stuff among us today!" The leaders of each of the twelve tribes relayed the critical instructions from God everyone would need to follow. None of them had made this trip before; they would need to trust God to show the way. Everyone was excited, but also anxious. They wanted to hear God's instructions and were all listening intently. The priests would carry the ark of the covenant, an earthly symbol of God dwelling with His people. Through the ark, God would reveal the way while the entire nation followed half a mile behind so they could see and react.

Now, crossing the Jordan in the spring is difficult for a handful of experienced people, and this was an entire nation. Even to this day, between heavy rain and melting mountain snow, the river floods and rages. So, more instructions were given to the priests who carried the ark. This was critical to the Israelites' success. When they reached the banks of the raging Jordan, they were to step into the water with the ark. When the priests stepped into the raging river, God promised, He would pile the water upstream "in a heap."

Inside the ark were the tablets of the Law, Aaron's rod, and a pot of manna—three precious reminders of God's presence. Not only would the priests be carrying this ark, but they'd also be half a mile from any military protection as every nearby nation spied on them. Priests leading the entire nation while separated from their nation's soldiers, carrying an ornate chest of precious items in a strange land they'd never visited, and stepping into a raging river—well, that's not stressful at all.

After they stepped into the water (not before), God cleared the riverbed. There they stood in the middle, with the ark, until every Israelite crossed the river safely—the entire nation! That wasn't fifteen minutes, mind you; it was a full day. The people recognized the connection to what God had done for Moses and their parents at the Red Sea. Together, they all witnessed evidence of God's presence, just like the story they'd heard of the Exodus.

THEOLOGY—UNITED BY GOD'S PRESENCE

The obvious miracle in this story was God stopping the flow of the Jordan, but that miracle couldn't have happened without a prior miracle: the Israelites' unified obedience to God's directions, everyone on the same page and walking the same path. This wasn't a handful of people, or even a hundred, but an entire nation of people—men, women, children, babies, and all their luggage.

Can you imagine what a disaster this operation would have been if they had not been unified in their obedience? What would have happened if some of them chose not to follow the priests and the ark? What if one of the tribes started advocating for a shortcut? "Meh, we'll find a safer way across the Jordan." What if another tribe said, "I think we'll just wait till after Passover; maybe then the river will be more passable!" What if those other tribes decided to bail on the whole concept of invading the promised land and stayed east of the Jordan? But, this wasn't the previous generation of complainers who always grumbled to Moses about God. None of them said, "Are you nuts, Joshua? We aren't following priests into that raging river!"

These priests weren't exactly experienced, trained wilderness guides, either, yet they were unified and followed God's commands. What was the catalyst for their unity? It was their collective faith and trust in His presence, represented by the ark. Specifically, the items carried inside the ark represented three attributes of His presence among His people.

God's Word

The law tablets given to Moses by God symbolized God's presence through His word. The Israelites' willingness to submit themselves to the law of God made them different from every other nation on earth. When the people and the priests heard the word of God given to Joshua, they trusted His word was true. By faith, everyone wanted to follow exactly what God said, and doing so kept them all unified on the same path.

God's Authority

But, why were they willing to trust and obey what Joshua said? Because they knew Joshua's authority came from God. This attribute of God's presence was symbolized by Aaron's rod. The story behind the rod is found in Numbers 17. When the time came for God to appoint representatives of His spiritual authority, He commanded one leader from each tribe to bring a staff to Moses, who put them inside the tabernacle overnight. If a staff sprouted flower buds, it meant that man and his tribe would be the representatives of God's spiritual authority. Aaron's staff was the one that bloomed. It became the symbol of God's complete authority over His people.

God's Provision

Obeying God's word and submitting to His authority isn't easy, especially when entering unknown territory. The bowl of manna in the ark was symbolic of God's faithfulness always to provide what His people need. God supplied the manna to His people for forty years in the wilderness. They always had everything they required.

You can see the ark was so much more to them than just a box of old relics; it was God's presence among His people. Faith in all three of these attributes of God's presence unified His people under one plan, behind one goal, on one path. They crossed the Jordan together with unified faith and reliance upon God's word, authority, and provision.

PERSONAL—CROSSING JORDAN TOGETHER

Even if the waters rage, there will be miraculous unity among those who follow the Lamb wherever He goes. I love how God brought an entire nation of people together in the perfect way at the perfect time—all the different opinions, agendas, personalities, concerns, goals, and hopes put in submission to God's plan! The Israelites' unity, miraculous as it was, stemmed from their shared faith and trust in those three attributes of God's presence. They were held together by a strong allegiance to God's word, His authority, and His provision.

Just like Israel, the church must metaphorically cross the Jordan into the land—that is, undertake the Great Commission. Our journey is a difficult journey. We don't really know the way, what will happen, or the obstacles faced. There's no way we can make that journey if we aren't unified like the nation of Israel was. If we try to go into the land without being unified, and everyone goes his or her own way, it's going to be a disaster.

So, how can we enjoy this same type of unity? What could we accomplish together for God? What will it take for us to have this kind of common purpose, especially when the waters are raging around us? Just like God led His people and carved a path for them through the ark of the covenant, He does the same for us. Our Ark is Jesus! He's the personification of God's word, authority, and provision:

Jesus is the Word of God. Revelation 19:13b says, "The name by which he is called is the Word of God."

Jesus has all authority. When the risen Jesus gave His apostles the Great Commission, Matthew 28:18 records, "Jesus came and said to them, 'All authority in heaven and on earth has been given to me.'"

Jesus is our provision. In Matthew 6:31–32, Jesus admonished us, "Do not be anxious, saying, 'What shall we eat?' or 'What shall we drink?' or 'What shall we wear?' For the pagans seek after all these things, and your heavenly Father knows that you need them all."

We *will* have miraculous unity when we obey God's word, yield to His authority, and trust in His provision. When we keep our eyes on our own Ark, our Jesus, we will experience that miraculous unity. It doesn't mean we'll always agree or that we won't have our own unique perspectives and insights. But, when we keep our eyes on our Ark, our differences become less important than our journey together. When we keep our eyes on Jesus before us, following Him wherever He goes, we will have one unified path. Remember Proverbs 3:5:

> *Trust in the LORD with all your heart and do not lean on your own understanding. In all your ways acknowledge him, and he will make straight your paths.*

Like the Israelites, we've never been this way before. Followers of Jesus know we desperately need God's presence to guide us. Just as God did for the nation of Israel, Jesus has given us specific instructions for our path into the land in the form of the Great Commission. He has provided us with a unified way into the land through His word, His power, and His provision. He gave us His word and told us what to teach. He also conferred spiritual authority, and He promised to be with us always, providing us with His presence. He has reassured us, as we read in Isaiah 43:2, "When you pass through the waters, I will be with you; and through the rivers, they shall not overwhelm you."

As we cross the Jordan into the promised land, we need everyone together, looking to Jesus to lead the way. Sometimes, the path He has commanded us to follow will not be the most comfortable; it may not even be safe. The raging waters will tempt us to take our eyes off Jesus to pursue personal goals, agendas, desires, and obsessions. We will be tempted to turn away from the presence of God for an easier, safer, or shorter path. Staying unified on His path would be easier if He calmed the roaring waters before we reached them, wouldn't it? But, consider that we're supposed to trust God's presence together, by faith, and step into the waters *before* He stops them. Trusting His word, His authority, and His provision will keep us unified as we go into the land, even if the waters rage.

Go into the Land!

CHAPTER SIX

Stones to Remember
(Joshua 4)

Have you ever experienced God's presence in a way that you would never forget, or at least never want to forget? Like the moment your eyes were opened to who you are and who Jesus is? That is a memorable, emotional experience. Maybe you experienced God's presence through a "just in time" provision of money, food, a friend, or good news. For some of us, we have experienced the unmistakable presence of God in moments of earthly crisis or catastrophe. As followers of Jesus, those moments when God manifests His presence in unforgettable ways are precious, removing any doubt God is real. No matter what life brings, you're certain you'll remember those moments.

But over time, inevitably, we do forget, don't we? We lose

faith and get discouraged; we isolate ourselves, wander, and lose our way. It's not because God's presence has left us. We have just forgotten, losing our awareness of His unchanging presence. That's why remembering what God has done for His people, and for you personally, is so important.

HISTORY—STONE MONUMENTS

On their way into the promised land, the Israelites built a physical reminder of their God story. But, this monument wasn't a product of human imagination. God gave them the idea in Joshua 4:1–7:

> *When all the nation had finished passing over the Jordan, the LORD said to Joshua, ² "Take twelve men, one from each tribe, ³ and command them, 'Take twelve stones out of the midst of the Jordan, from the place where the priests' feet stood firmly, and bring them over with you and lay them down in the place where you lodge tonight.'" ⁴ Then Joshua called the twelve men from the people of Israel, whom he had appointed. ⁵ And Joshua said to them, "Pass before the ark of the LORD your God into the midst of the Jordan, and take up each of you a stone upon his shoulder, according to the number of the tribes of the people of Israel, ⁶ that this may be a sign among you. When your children ask in time to come, 'What do those stones mean to you?' ⁷ then you shall tell them that the waters of the Jordan were cut off before the ark of the covenant of the LORD. When it passed over the Jordan, the waters of the*

Jordan were cut off. So these stones shall be to the people of Israel a memorial forever."

The entire nation had just witnessed and received an undeniable, miraculous manifestation of God's presence. Crossing the Jordan was a pivotal moment that future generations would need to remember and celebrate together. So, God directed one man from each tribe to go back into the dry riverbed where the priests stood and pick out a large stone. These were stones big enough to be carried out on their shoulders; they wouldn't be easily moved or washed away. The twelve stones were arranged together in a monument clearly visible to anyone walking that way for generations thereafter.

It was a quite simple monument, not grandiose like a crystal cathedral, gaudy temple, expensive statue, or grand architectural wonder. It wasn't like the monuments the world builds to glorify itself, such as the Egyptian pyramids. But, it served its purpose: reminding God's people, and others, what He had done for the Israelites.

Then, Joshua told the Israelites to find twelve more stones and stack those in the middle of the riverbed where the priests stood. This, too, would be visible to those passing by, obstructing the flowing water in the river no matter the season. One monument marked the spot where God parted the water, the other where the people celebrated God's faithfulness. One creating an obvious water feature in the river, the other a clearly manmade rock monument on land. These two simple, durable monuments weren't built for the generation

Joshua led, who would never forget that day. They were for future generations of children and grandchildren to see, prompting them to ask their elders what those stone piles stood for.

THEOLOGY—HOW GOD USES STONES

The Israelites obeyed God's command to build a monument of stones. In Joshua 4:8–9, Joshua had them construct two monuments:

> *The people did just as Joshua commanded and took up twelve stones out of the Jordan, one for each tribe, just as the LORD told Joshua. They carried them over with them to the place where they lodged and laid them down there. ⁹ Joshua set up twelve stones in the midst of the Jordan, in the place where the feet of the priests bearing the ark of the covenant had stood; and they are there to this day.*

God knew, left on their own, His people would tend to remember only what He had done for them lately. God knows how easily we forget His faithfulness, including the big moments and those that happen in our own lives! For example, one generation earlier had experienced the first Passover, the Exodus, crossing the Red Sea, the pillar of fire at night and the cloud for shade by day, and the daily manna—all incredible manifestations of God's presence. Do you think if we experienced those things today, our faith would be encouraged? We would never forget, right? I bet left on our own, we would. The Israelites forgot. They still found reasons to doubt Him and complain He had forgotten them.

God knows how important it is for His people to remember what He has done for them. He knows we need reminders! So God gave them these two monuments to do two important things to help them remember and proclaim His faithfulness.

Stones to Remind

After the Israelites had crossed the Jordan River, Joshua ensured the Israelites built the monument there as God had commanded. Better yet, in Joshua 4:20–24, he made sure they knew what this pile of stones commemorated:

> *And those twelve stones, which they took out of the Jordan, Joshua set up at Gilgal. ^{21} And said to the people of Israel, "When your children ask their fathers in times to come, 'What do these stones mean?' ^{22} then you shall let your children know, 'Israel passed over this Jordan on dry ground.' ^{23} For the LORD your God dried up the waters of the Jordan for you until you passed over, as the LORD your God did to the Red Sea, which He dried up for us until we passed over, ^{24} so that all the peoples of the earth may know that the hand of the LORD is mighty, [so] that you may fear the LORD your God forever."*

The two monuments would remind future generations about precisely what God did for them at the Jordan River.

God made it clear: "You will construct these so that future generations can be taught about My faithfulness. They need to know that I am the way, the truth, and the life, and I will always be with them!" Families would make a pilgrimage to Gilgal and let the children see the objects. These young Israelites would ask their elders, "What are these rocks on the shore and in the river for? Who put them there?"

And the grown-ups would reply, "Let me tell you about the day God made His presence known to us through His word, His authority, and His provision. Then God told us to build a monument for you—yes, He was thinking of you that day as well! He wanted to make sure you know how He feels about you, because you were so young (or not born yet)."

God's commands to Joshua and the Israelites to pile stones in remembrance were similar to what Jesus commanded His disciples at their last supper together, the night before He died. In Luke 22:17–20, Jesus told them to make a monument to Him through bread and wine:

> *And he took a cup, and when he had given thanks he said, "Take this, and divide it among yourselves. [18] For I tell you that from now on I will not drink of the fruit of the vine until the kingdom of God comes." [19] And he took bread, and when he had given thanks, he broke it and gave it to them, saying, "This is my body, which is given for you. Do this in remembrance of me." [20] And likewise the cup after they had eaten, saying, "This cup that is poured out for you is the new covenant in my blood.*

Stones to Proclaim

Also, God wants every nation on earth to know who He is and the remarkable things He has done for their salvation. Those monuments became a way to proclaim to the nations what God does for those who obey and follow Him. Can you see the obvious link here to the Great Commission, our mandate to proclaim to all nations everything Jesus taught us?

Living Stones

In our church sanctuary, the steps to our stage are built of Jerusalem stone. That's cool, right? Well, yes, it's cool, but these earthly stones won't last forever. (They almost didn't make it through our last renovation!)

God used two monuments built by human hands from twelve stones to memorialize His grace and love to His people. I also love how God specifically used twelve stones, one for each tribe, making it a monument for the entire nation. The book of Revelation uses the number 12 as a metaphor for the entirety of all God's people throughout all redemptive history. (See Revelation 7:5–8.) Those stone monuments served their purpose, but they couldn't last forever. They were never intended to be a permanent monument to God's faithfulness, grace, and mercy for His people. This is what Jesus meant when He said, in Mark 14:58, He would destroy the temple in Jerusalem and build a new one:

> *We heard him say, "I will destroy this temple that is made with hands, and in three days I will build another not made with hands."*

Thankfully, since about 33 AD, God has been building a new monument to His grace and mercy with stones that *will* last forever. And where are the stones? Who are the stones? We are! He's built a monument out of His people, as 1 Peter 2:5 explains:

> *You yourselves like living stones are being built up as a spiritual house...*

See, the stones Israel used were just dead rocks. But we, those who follow the Lamb, are a living monument—an eternal, mobile, organic, biblical, generous monument, far superior to a pile of dead stones or a temple. We are living stones, monuments to God's miraculous grace, mercy, and power, who have become witnesses to all nations! Jesus has made us a monument built from living stones, both where He lives and in the raging river of this world.

Personal—God's New Monuments

The greatest monument to God's faithfulness isn't built by men from stone or brick; it's the one Jesus has built. When we forget God's grace and mercy, it's because we have become too distracted, obsessed with this present world. Raging rivers around us have grabbed most, if not all, our attention: politics, money, our personal struggles, fear, and anxiety.

Do you forget about God's power, grace, and mercy far too readily? It's easy to do in the comfort of America. We often turn to God as a last resort. We become self-sufficient. We wander, disconnecting from the monument of living stones God is building. The more disconnected you become from God's monument of living stones, His people, the harder it is to remember what God has done and is doing. Not only that, but you will also begin to lose hope in what God has promised He will do. You'll have a spiritual crisis! You will become resentful, angry, bitter, anxious, all because you have neglected the monuments to what God has done.

In Ephesians 2:12–13, Paul encouraged believers to remember the night-and-day difference between life apart from Jesus and life as a living stone:

> *Remember that you [Gentiles] were at that time separated from Christ, alienated from the people of God, and strangers to the covenants of promise, having no hope and without God in the world. ¹³ But now in Christ Jesus you who once were far off have been brought near by the blood of Christ.*

In other words, Paul said, "If you want to remain faithful, follow the Lamb wherever He goes and live among the monuments to what God has done. Those who are young in faith need to learn what Jesus has done in the lives of believers. Learn about all God has done for His people and His new monuments. Those who have experienced God's faithfulness need to share their stories! We need to proclaim to them stories of God's faithfulness to His church for two thousand years so they will be ready. You need to tell them about what Jesus has done—how He changed your life through the gospel of Jesus. Tell them how there will be raging waters, temptations, trials, hardships that will test their faith and tempt them to stray. Tell them there will be times when they want to wander from the monument He's building, to go it alone and make their own path. But we are God's monument to these lessons so they won't forget when the rivers of life rage around them."

Notice that the Israelites constructed two monuments, one in the river and one where they camped on the far side. That's exactly what Jesus had in mind when He instructed us to build a second monument of our own. But, we don't stack dead stones into statues or cathedrals. Our second monument is fellowship (or communion) around the Lord's table, as Paul explained in 1 Corinthians 11:24–26:

> *And when he had given thanks, he broke it [the bread] and said, "This is my body, which is for you. Do this in remembrance of me."* [25] *In the same way also he took the cup, after supper, saying, "This cup is the new covenant in my blood. Do this as often as you drink it, in remembrance of me."* [26] *For as often as you eat this bread and drink the cup, you proclaim the Lord's death until he comes.*

The outside world may have seen the Israelites' pile of rocks as trivial, or maybe they came to resent the reminder of

God's people coming to claim the promised land. It's how the world sees the monuments we have today, baptism and the Lord's table. But, these monuments to God stories, past and present, are precious to His people.

Like the monument of stones at Gilgal, the Lord's table is designed for remembering and proclaiming. Only, instead of stacking rocks one time, the Lord's table allows us to build a monument to His glory each time we participate. It points us back to what Jesus did for us on the cross, a tangible reminder for us and future generations of what Jesus has done, even when the rivers of life rage around us.

CHAPTER SEVEN

A Fresh Start
(Joshua 5:1–12)

We all love a fresh start, a sense of hope and renewal, especially when we are carrying the burden of failure. Have you ever felt like you needed a fresh start spiritually? What did you do to try to achieve that fresh start? Is there a fresh start checklist or standard procedure?

Many of us start by making a firm new commitment to change old habits and take a new direction. Or, we might declare it's time to end particular, toxic relationships. Such things certainly may be *evidence* of a fresh start, but they aren't how it begins.

How many of your fresh starts have started well but failed? Why didn't they last? Too many attempts at new beginnings lack the power to truly transform. Many people see a fresh start as something we accomplish through our own individual efforts, but a true fresh start doesn't begin alone. "Be the change you want to see" offers empty hope, a mirage without substance or power to make a real difference.

For followers of Jesus, the only way to a true fresh start is in community, loving relentlessly through unified obedience to God. Any attempt at a fresh start based on mere individual effort is a form of self-righteousness, an expression only of belief in your own ability to bring about lasting spiritual transformation. Jesus gave us two powerful symbols, which I mentioned in Chapter Six, that show the power of unified obedience in community for providing a fresh start: communion at the Lord's table and baptism. They're connected to the act of obedience Joshua and the Israelites undertook at God's command in Joshua 5:1–3:

> *As soon as all the kings of the Amorites who were beyond the Jordan to the west, and all the kings of the Canaanites who were by the sea, heard that the LORD had dried up the waters of the Jordan for the people of Israel until they had crossed over, their hearts melted and there was no longer any spirit in them because of the people of Israel. ² At that time the LORD said to Joshua, "Make flint knives and circumcise the sons of Israel a second time." ³ So Joshua made flint knives and circumcised the sons of Israel at Gibeath-haaraloth.*

HISTORY—
A NEW BEGINNING FOR GOD'S PEOPLE

It had been forty years since Moses led Israel out of Egypt. So much had transpired since then! They had been wandering for four decades, both physically and spiritually. Despite stunning examples of God's presence and favor, that generation became complacent, entitled spiritual brats. They believed they were entitled to all the benefits of being God's people without the responsibilities that come with it, so they spent forty years complaining constantly to Moses. They weren't happy with the way God chose to deliver and provide for them, and their lack of gratitude led to disobedience. They began to drift toward idolatry, like worshiping a golden calf. Obedience to God's commands, like observing Passover, began to fade. The first anniversary of Passover was celebrated (Numbers 9), but then there's no other mention until here, in Joshua 5.

The Israelites had also neglected the circumcision of newborn males, the most important earthly sign they were part of God's covenant. Joshua 5:4–7 explains this and emphasizes the connection between circumcision and obedience:

> *And this is the reason why Joshua circumcised them: all the males of the people who came out of Egypt, all the men of war, had died in the wilderness on the way after they had come out of Egypt.* ⁵ *Though all the people who came out had been circumcised, yet all the people who were born on the way in the wilderness after they had come out of Egypt had not been circumcised.* ⁶ *For*

> *the people of Israel walked forty years in the wilderness until all the nation, the men of war who came out of Egypt, perished because they did not obey the voice of the LORD; the LORD swore to them that he would not let them see the land that the LORD had sworn to their fathers to give to us, a land flowing with milk and honey.* ⁷ *So it was their children whom he raised up in their place that Joshua circumcised. For they were uncircumcised because they had not been circumcised on the way.*

Understand, circumcision and Passover were not frivolous, ceremonial dogma you'd expect religious-minded people to participate in. These were observances designed to set them apart clearly from the rest of the nations on the earth. It's similar to how many churches today drift from the true gospel and other teachings of Jesus they find burdensome. The breadth and depth of the Israelites' disobedience was so pervasive, God declared them a lost generation in Numbers 14:27–30:

> *How long shall this wicked congregation grumble against me? . . .* ²⁹ *Your dead bodies shall fall in this wilderness, and of all your number, listed in the census from twenty years old and upward, who have grumbled against me,* ³⁰ *not one shall come into the land where I swore that I would make you dwell, except Caleb and Joshua the son of Nun.*

When that older generation passed, God appointed Moses' apprentice, Joshua, as the new leader for His people. God parted the Jordan River for them, showing them His continued presence and favor just as He had with Moses. This younger generation was unified in their obedience to God's instructions even when those commands defied earthly logic. They weren't perfect (as we'll see later), but they weren't the entitled complainers their parents had been. Their faith translated into action; together in faith, they crossed the Jordan into the promised land. But, there were remnants of unfinished business, because they still carried the consequences of the previous generation's rebellion. They needed a fresh start, which would come with the reinstatement of God's commands regarding circumcision and the Passover feast.

THEOLOGY—THE COVENANT RENEWED

God wanted their first act of obedience in the promised land to be a visible symbol of the renewal of the covenant He made with their parents, the covenant He kept despite the previous generation's whining rebellion and neglect. In Joshua 5:8–12, the Israelites obeyed God's commands and He confirmed their fresh start:

> *When the circumcising of the whole nation was finished, they remained in their places in the camp until they were healed.* ⁹ *And the LORD said to Joshua, "Today I have rolled away the reproach of Egypt from you." And so the name of that place is called Gilgal to this day.*

> *[10] While the people of Israel were encamped at Gilgal, they kept the Passover on the fourteenth day of the month in the evening on the plains of Jericho. [11] And the day after the Passover, on that very day, they ate of the produce of the land, unleavened cakes and parched grain. [12] And the manna ceased the day after they ate of the produce of the land. There was no longer manna for the people of Israel, but they ate of the fruit of the land of Canaan that year.*

In unified obedience, the Israelites renewed these two covenant signs, circumcision and Passover, demonstrating they were God's people. It was the same as our obedience to the commands Jesus gave us regarding the two signs of the new covenant. Let's explore how circumcision and Passover are connected directly to baptism and the Lord's table.

From Circumcision to Baptism

Circumcision was a visible mark of the Israelites' commitment to God's covenant, an outward sign of an inward transformation. Circumcision was meant to display permanent identification with the people of God. That's what baptism is, as Paul explained in Colossians 2:11–13:

> *In him also you were circumcised with a circumcision made without hands, by putting off the body of the flesh, by the circumcision of Christ, [12] having been buried with him in baptism, in which you were also raised with him through faith in the powerful working of God, who raised him from the dead. [13] And you, who were dead in your trespasses and the uncircumcision of*

your flesh, God made alive together with him, having forgiven us all our trespasses...

Their obedience to this first command might seem unnecessary, even risky, from an earthly perspective. Circumcising every male put them out of commission for a couple of days, vulnerable to potential attack. But, unlike their parents, this generation had faith and trust that led directly to their unified obedience. It was a precious renewal of commitment to the covenant with God, a separation from the rebellious legacy of their parents. It wasn't some pointless ritual; it was a powerful, faith-driven expression in the name of God, just like baptism. God's command for circumcision in Joshua 5 is connected directly to that command Jesus gave us in the Great Commission, in Matthew 28:19–20:

Go therefore and make disciples of all nations, baptizing them in the name of the Father and of the Son and of the Holy Spirit, [20] teaching them to observe all that I have commanded you...

From Passover to Jesus, the Lamb of God

The second command, to reinstate Passover, marked the Israelites' transition from being wanderers to being people in a new land, with a purpose. Did you know Jesus intended the first Lord's table He celebrated with His disciples to be a replacement for Passover? That first communion was on the night of Passover. Jesus made it clear He was the Lamb of God and Passover was no longer about remembering Exodus, but about gathering to remember and celebrate the cross.

When a church community today celebrates the New Covenant Passover together, it's a remembrance in unified obedience after the example Jesus set.

From the End of the Manna to Jesus, the Bread of Life

Tucked away at the end of Joshua 5 is this juicy theological morsel: God stopped sending the manna every morning. The land they were about to inherit would provide everything they needed for life and obedience—food way better than manna!

In the New Testament, Jesus taught His followers He is the sustenance better than any food. He described Himself as the "bread of life" in John 6:32–35:

> *"Truly, truly, I say to you, it was not Moses who gave you the bread from heaven, but my Father gives you the true bread from heaven. ^{33} For the bread of God is he who comes down from heaven and gives life to the world."... ^{35} Jesus said to them, "I am the bread of life; whoever comes to me shall not hunger, and whoever believes in me shall never thirst."*

You know, it's not just a throwaway line when Jesus taught us to pray to God for our daily bread. Every part of this story in Joshua about circumcision and Passover foreshadows Jesus and the symbols of the new, better covenant God has made with us, His people.

PERSONAL—KEEPING IT FRESH

What do you think would have happened if fifty percent of the Israelite men had said, "Nah, I am not doing the circumcision thing"? Looking around and seeing unified obedience to these Old Testament symbols created a powerful, encouraging community of faith. They didn't see this as individuals being circumcised or celebrating Passover. It was the entire nation of God doing these things together. Their unified obedience in circumcision and Passover brought joy! It reminded them that faith is not something we are supposed to pursue alone; it's a community thing. This is the same impact we feel when we participate in the New Covenant versions of circumcision and Passover—baptism and the Lord's table.

Too many Christians see a fresh start as merely a personal choice or commitment. Need a fresh start with God? The first step to a new beginning is being part of a community of unified, obedient believers. It's a community achievement. It's not born from a motivational speech that inspires you, but from a community in unified obedience. No matter how hard you try, you'll never have true renewal on your own. It *must* start with community. Individually, our fresh start will only be as real as the one your community provides. Unified obedience in community inspires true repentance, forgiveness, humility, transformation, and renewal.

Jesus knew we would need to be reminded of the importance of being in unified obedience in community. That's why He commanded we partake in, and celebrate, two symbols of the New Covenant together: the new Passover (communion at the Lord's table) and the new circumcision (baptism). Paul explained in Colossians 2:12–13:

> ... *having been buried with him in baptism, in which you were also raised with him through faith in the powerful working of God, who raised him from the dead. ¹³ And you, who were dead in your trespasses and the uncircumcision of your flesh, God made alive together with him, having forgiven us all our trespasses.*

Like circumcision, baptism is not some religious hoop to jump through, a task to mark off your list. Remember how circumcision at Gilgal symbolized a transition from the wilderness and the rebellion of their parents? Baptism is a community expression of the circumcision of our hearts, symbolizing a transition from the old to the new. Our old self, like that older generation of Israelites, has passed away. Paul wrote in Romans 6:4:

> *We were buried therefore with him by baptism into death, in order that just as Christ was raised from the dead by the glory of the Father, we too might walk in newness of life.*

See why baptism was never intended as something done privately with only friends and family? It's an expression of the joy we have in our renewal and our passionate desire to identify with Christ and His people. Baptism, like the Lord's table, is a community event. Like circumcision and Passover for the Israelites, these celebrations proclaim a new, obedient, faithful creation has come to life in unified obedience within a community of God's people!

Go into the Land!

CHAPTER EIGHT

Is God on Your Side?
(Joshua 5:13–15)

Have you ever wondered if God is on your side? Have you asked yourself, "Is God really for me?" You might feel unsure whether it's okay even to ask that question; yet, it sure seems like a lot of other people have it a lot easier. The question seems preposterous from a certain angle. If we genuinely believe our Jesus is in control, why would we question whose side He's on? Of course, we prefer—even expect—God's side to align with ours, for His plans to mesh with our plans.

But, we need a unique perspective, especially given this daily battle we're part of, between evil and righteousness. Wondering and questioning what side Jesus is on becomes irrelevant when you consider the stakes of that contest. So, let me post a different question: if we truly follow the Lamb wherever He goes, should we even have our own side?

We abandoned our side when we became followers of Jesus. For us, only one side prevails, only one side leads to victory, and that is His side. That makes our side irrelevant, so expecting God to be on our side is misguided. Instead, we ought to be asking, "Am I on Your side, Jesus?"

In Joshua 5:13–15, the leader of the Israelites met someone unexpected and, inadvertently, found himself asking whose side God was on:

> *When Joshua was by Jericho, he lifted up his eyes and looked, and behold, a man was standing before him with his drawn sword in his hand. And Joshua went to him and said to him, "Are you for us or for our adversaries?"* [14] *And he said, "No; but I am the commander of the army of the LORD. Now I have come." And Joshua fell on his face to the earth and worshiped and said to him, "What does my lord say to his servant?"* [15] *And the commander of the LORD's army said to Joshua, "Take off your sandals from your feet, for the place where you are standing is holy." And Joshua did so.*

HISTORY—ARE YOU FOR US OR AGAINST US?

Joshua and the nation of Israel stood at a pivotal moment in their history. Having crossed the Jordan River, they found themselves on the precipice of the promised land. A sense of renewal and divine presence permeated the atmosphere as they reinstated the sacred symbols of their covenant with God, the rituals of circumcision and Passover. Their first significant military challenge, the conquest of Jericho, awaited them.

Jericho wasn't the largest city in Canaan but had a reputation for its towering walls and formidable defenses. Most nations, especially an unseasoned force like the Israelites, wouldn't even bother to invade Jericho. Yet, conquering Jericho was a critical first step for God's people. Success was crucial to ensure there wouldn't be attacks from the rear as they ventured deeper into the promised land. Controlling Jericho would also provide strategic access to the central and southern parts of Canaan.

Taking this first city was critical not just militarily but psychologically, too. The Canaanites were already afraid; this would cement their fears. It would also be a huge morale booster and further affirm their faith in God to give them victory.

I can imagine Joshua pacing and worrying, wrestling with the weight of his responsibility. Despite the tangible signs of God's presence and favor, he could feel the pressure of the forthcoming battle. Walking around the outskirts of Jericho deep in thought, strategizing and seeking divine guidance through prayer, Joshua looked up and was startled by the unexpected sight of a man of battle.

This man's formidable appearance suggested he was not someone you'd want to face on the battlefield. Joshua's question, "Are you for us or for our adversaries?" indicates he didn't yet know who this man was. Otherwise, he wouldn't have asked that question but something more like, "What do You want me to do? Just tell me. Here am I; send me."

The man revealed to Joshua that He wasn't on either side, because He was the commander of the army of the Lord. He wasn't there to help Israel, but rather to fight the battle on their behalf with the army of God! The real question wasn't which side He was on; it was which side Israel was on.

Joshua made it clear which side he chose by falling flat on his face, now recognizing the divine authority who had chosen to appear before him. Joshua was filled with a mixture of awe, reverence, worship, and importantly, confidence. The commander told Joshua to take his sandals off, a beautiful echo of Moses' encounter with God in Exodus 3:4–5:

> *God called to him out of the bush, "Moses, Moses!" And he said, "Here I am." ⁵ Then he said, "Do not come near; take your sandals off your feet, for the place on which you are standing is holy ground."*

The biblical concept of holy ground is always a reference to a place where God's presence is manifested. Understand, the patch of ground itself wasn't special; it was made special by the presence of God. That patch of ground was holy because He was standing on it—and His holy presence has that effect.

THEOLOGY—COMMANDER JESUS

No doubt, this commander who appeared to Joshua was our Jesus. There are many ways we know this, but the clearest is found in several undeniable links between the books of Joshua and Revelation, specifically the parallels of Joshua's encounter to John's interaction with Jesus.

A Sword for Judgment

In Joshua, the commander of the Lord's army held a drawn sword representing pending judgment on Jericho. In Revelation, Jesus had a sharp, double-edged sword in His mouth, the one He will use when He returns to judge all evil. John described Jesus and His sword in Revelation 1:16:

> *In his right hand he held seven stars, from his mouth came a sharp two-edged sword, and his face was like the sun shining in full strength.*

Humble Worship

Have you ever had an unexpected spiritual encounter with Jesus? It's a supernatural phenomenon, and you can't help but respond to Him with worship in a way only other followers of Jesus could understand.

Similarly, Joshua's response to the presence of the commander was to fall on his face in worship, recognizing who He was. This was not a planned worship service but an instinctive, reactive kind of worship. John seemed to have the exact same instinct when Jesus appeared to him in Revelation 1:17–18:

> *When I saw him, I fell at his feet as though dead. But he laid his right hand on me, saying, "Fear not, I am*

the first and the last, 18 and the living one. I died, and behold, I am alive forevermore, and I have the keys of Death and Hades."

For more proof, see the contrast with Revelation 22:8–9, when John was overwhelmed by everything he'd been shown and fell to the ground before the angel:

And when I heard and saw them, I fell down to worship at the feet of the angel who showed them to me, ⁹ but he said to me, "You must not do that! I am a fellow servant with you and your brothers the prophets and with those who keep the words of this book. Worship God."

In this case, the angel in Revelation told John, "Don't worship me. I'm just an angel!" The commander didn't say that to Joshua because He was Jesus, the same Jesus whom John saw in Revelation 1 and who allowed both men to worship Him accordingly.

An Important Commission

Both Joshua and John received assurance, Joshua about Jericho and John about the triumph of God's kingdom over evil. Both men experienced a surprising, breathtaking, unplanned encounter with Jesus resulting in instinctive worship. Filled with humble confidence after meeting Jesus, Joshua and John were both given an important commission to fulfill. Joshua was to lead the Israelites to victory in the battle of Jericho, while Jesus told John to write down everything he was about to see so everyone who read it could be blessed.

PERSONAL—
FOLLOWERS OF JESUS DON'T HAVE A SIDE

When facing challenges, do you want God on your side, or do you want to be on His? Which way would give you greater confidence? Consider Joshua's and John's respective encounters with Jesus. Once Joshua saw who was really leading the battle—and it wasn't him—he knew everything would be just fine. Once John received the beautiful revelation of Jesus, I imagine he began writing it down as furiously as he could!

Obviously, we aren't Joshua or John; we haven't seen Jesus face to face. Yet, as followers of Jesus, we have met Him. The Jesus they met is the same Jesus you met when He called you out of darkness to follow Him wherever He goes. When you met Jesus, it wasn't just for forgiveness of sins, to straighten out your life, or so you could go to heaven when you die. You were also given a commission to follow your commander, Jesus, wherever He goes, bringing the gospel to all the nations. In Matthew 12:30, He drew clear battle lines for His followers:

> *Whoever is not with me is against me, and whoever does not gather with me scatters.*

The picture of Joshua's encounter with Jesus sheds a whole new light on those words He said in Matthew. Those of us who have truly met Him understand Joshua's humble reverence for Him. It's not born from fear or anxiety; it's a sense of humility born out of the immensity of our gratitude. Your humble worship, inspired by the day you met Him, will cure you from the narcissistic cancer of obsession with your perceived self-interest. It inspires you to abandon "your side," run to His side, and follow Him wherever He goes.

Now, if we worship Him this way even though we haven't seen His face, can you imagine our response when we do? There will come a day when we do see Jesus, just as Joshua did near Jericho and John did on Patmos. Jesus will be holding that sword of His word, and He will use it to bring an end the age-old war between good and evil. In that moment, we will fall to our faces before Him, overjoyed and overwhelmed by His breath-taking presence.

Until that day, the power of His word will be our shield, His spirit will be our confidence, and His people will be our inspiration. Until then, we will follow our commander wherever He leads, into all the nations, with the gospel. That's being on His side.

CHAPTER NINE

Six Days of Trumpets
(Joshua 6:1–14)

For some people, trumpets bring to mind the band Chicago, jazz trumpeter Louis Armstrong, or other modern musicians who are easy on the ears. Do you know what trumpets make me think about? Loud, obnoxious fanfares, just because some narcissist entered a room.

In fact, trumpets were the loudest manmade sound in the ancient world. They were unnerving to adversaries, often used for shock and awe impact. For many, a trumpet fanfare can be an irritant—disturbing, distracting, and painful if you're standing too close. The best part about blaring trumpets is when they stop, especially if they're coming from your enemy.

But, the same blast of trumpets may be inspiring to the trumpeters' allies. If you can hear trumpets, you're still alive; if you are no longer among the living, you won't hear them no matter how loud they are. Trumpets can also mean help is on the way. As annoying as they are, if you hear trumpets and understand their significance, hope remains.

Trumpets played a critical part in God's plan for the defeat of Jericho, as He explained in Joshua 6:1–5:

> *Now Jericho was shut up inside and outside because of the people of Israel. None went out and none came in. ² And the LORD said to Joshua, "See, I have given Jericho into your hand, with its king and mighty men of valor. ³ You shall march around the city, all the men of war going around the city once. Thus shall you do for six days. ⁴ Seven priests shall bear seven trumpets of rams' horns before the ark. On the seventh day you shall march around the city seven times, and the priests shall blow the trumpets. ⁵ When they make a long blast with the ram's horn, when you hear the sound of the trumpet, then all the people shall shout with a great shout, and the wall of the city will fall down flat, and the people shall go up, everyone straight before him."*

History—A Strange Strategy

Obedience Without All the Answers

Put yourself in the place of the groups of people on either side of this odd military tactic. First, the Israelites, who had been amping up for this battle. They knew it wouldn't be easy, but they were fired up and ready to go. Jericho was an infamous, well-protected fortress city, not just with its massive walls but also with a mighty fighting force. God's plan? The army would hold a praise march around the city once a day for six days, then take the rest of the day off. One trip around the city would have taken Israel's army maybe thirty minutes to an hour. Directly behind their marching ranks were seven priests blowing seven trumpets with the ark of the covenant (God's presence) in tow. The soldiers marching in front of the priests' horns and the ark were not supposed to speak. That was their job for six days. Can you imagine how bizarre these instructions must have seemed? "Okay, God, we'll do it," the Israelites responded, "but we don't understand why." They followed God's instructions the way Joshua relayed them, in Joshua 6:9–14:

> *So Joshua the son of Nun called the priests and said to them, "Take up the ark of the covenant and let seven priests bear seven trumpets of rams' horns before the ark of the LORD."* [7] *And he said to the people, "Go forward. March around the city and let the armed men pass on before the ark of the LORD."* [8] *And just as Joshua had commanded the people, the seven priests bearing the seven trumpets of rams' horns before the LORD went forward, blowing the trumpets, with the ark of the covenant of the LORD following them.* [9] *The armed men were walking before the priests who were blowing the trumpets, and the rear guard was walking after the ark while the trumpets blew continually.* [10] *But Joshua commanded the people, "You shall not*

shout or make your voice heard, neither shall any word go out of your mouth until the day I tell you to shout. Then you shall shout." ¹¹ *So he caused the ark of the* LORD *to circle the city, going about it once. And they came into the camp and spent the night in the camp.*

¹² *Then Joshua rose early in the morning, and the priests took up the ark of the* LORD. ¹³ *And the seven priests bearing the seven trumpets of rams' horns before the ark of the* LORD *walked on, and they blew the trumpets continually. The armed men were walking before them, and the rear guard was walking after the ark of the* LORD *while the trumpets blew continually.* ¹⁴ *And the second day they marched around the city once and returned into the camp. So they did for six days.*

Do you ever feel confused as a follower of Jesus? You're willing to do what God says, but His directions sure are baffling. The Israelites' obedience to this strange battle plan was an act of faith, just like crossing the Jordan River.

Living With Trumpets

What about the people inside Jericho? They were already full of anxiety, and then came day one of the trumpets and marching. "The day we have feared is here!" Thirty minutes later, they watched Israel's army leave and return to their tents for the day. "Wait, that was it? We don't see any siege equipment. Where are the ramps, ropes, and ladders? Are they just scouting our weaknesses? Maybe they decided not to attack us; they think the walls are too strong. Maybe we're off the hook!" But, Israel came back a second day, with the same quiet army leading seven trumpeting priests and the ark once around the city. This bizarre scene repeated for six days.

I wonder if around day three, the people of Jericho started getting a little comfortable. Maybe their confidence in the walls started to grow. Maybe they believed they didn't need to fear Israel anymore. "Is this their plan? A silent army leading priests playing trumpets while carrying that stupid box everywhere they go?" Maybe they started in with some trash talk from atop their walls. Our world gets that way about God sometimes, doesn't it? As the gospel is preached, and we proclaim His grace and mercy as well as warnings of His judgment, it seems silly to many people. Yet, His word, grace, mercy, and judgment are no less real.

THEOLOGY—HOW GOD USES TRUMPETS

Obviously, God could have brought the walls of Jericho down on the very first day, but He didn't do that. Why did God make Israel go through six days of trumpet-filled, ark-toting trips around Jericho? This entire story, just like the commander who appeared in Joshua 5, is linked directly to the book of Revelation. In Revelation chapters 8 to 11, John described six trumpets bringing hail, fire, blood, and other calamities as metaphorical warnings of God's judgment. Jericho foreshadowed those warning trumpets.

Trumpets to Warn

The Israelites' unconventional siege of Jericho was connected to a promise God made to their ancestor Abraham centuries earlier, in Genesis 15:13–16:

> The LORD said to Abram, "Know for certain that your offspring will be sojourners in a land that is not theirs and will be slaves there, and they will be afflicted for four hundred years. ¹⁴ But I will bring judgment on the nation that they serve, and afterward they shall come out with great possessions.... ¹⁶ And they shall come back here in the fourth generation, for the iniquity of the Amorites [or Canaanites] is not yet complete."

That promise contained grace for the Israelites, but also for the Canaanites. Although Egypt would enslave his descendants for four hundred years, God promised Abraham they'd return to Canaan one day. But first, they'd have to wait, because the Canaanites' sin was "not yet full." God's grace is a long game. Later, we'll learn how deep the evil and wickedness among the people living in Jericho and the rest of Canaan became. (It was bad.) They knew who God was, because before their Egyptian captivity, Abraham and his people lived among the people in Canaan. For hundreds of years, the Canaanites had a standing invitation to repent and join God's covenant with Israel, like Rahab did.

Now God gave Jericho six final days of trumpets as their final warning. See how the trumpets displayed God's mercy? For six days they had the chance, like Rahab and her family, to trust God and join His people, yet they ignored the trumpets. They didn't abandon their love for Jericho, their way of life, or their trust in those huge walls built with human hands.

The first six trumpets in Revelation 8 to 11 were also designed to provide a final warning to the inhabitants of the earth. Those trumpets serve as warnings for the inevitable, hopeless cycle of failure and calamity plaguing human history. They reveal how anything humans build ultimately fails and how foolish it is to place our hope in our own endeavors. These trumpets, sounding throughout our age of the church and the gospel, are also one final, merciful call to abandon earthly hope and join God's people. Just like at Jericho, a seventh day of trumpets is coming, and time is running out. Sadly, most people are like the citizens of Jericho and won't abandon their hope in the things they love about this world. Revelation 9:20–21 describes this futile attachment:

> *The rest of mankind, who were not killed by these plagues, did not repent of the works of their hands nor give up worshiping demons or idols of gold, silver, bronze, stone, and wood, which cannot see or hear or walk. ²¹ Nor did they repent of their murders or their sorceries or their sexual immorality or their thefts.*

The six metaphorical trumpets we hear today get louder, as does the passionate resentment of those ignoring them, as the sounding of the seventh trumpet draws closer.

Trumpets to Encourage

For us, those first six trumpets in Revelation, like the Israelites' trumpets at Jericho, remind God's people this battle belongs to Him. Both sets of trumpets precede victory for God's people, whether the fall of Jericho to Joshua's army or the fall of evil in this world to Jesus. Just as He promised to show up for Israel on the seventh day, He has promised to return for us with His seventh trumpet! (See Revelation 11:15–19.) As long as the trumpets sound their warning, we're inspired to invite the world to join us as we follow Jesus faithfully. We proclaim the gospel of mercy as the only hope that won't fail on the day our Jesus returns with the seventh trumpet.

PERSONAL—CAN YOU HEAR THE TRUMPETS?

There are two important personal applications to consider in this part of Joshua's story: our mission and God's mercy. Remember how God asked Joshua and the Israelites to wait through six days of trumpets, based on the promise of a seventh? The same is true for us as followers of Jesus. We are told to wait out Revelation's six trumpets based on the promise of a seventh. These trumpets are a beautiful metaphor for how Jesus uses the gospel today. Loud trumpets are annoying; but, as long as you still hear them, there's time to follow Jesus!

Just like the Israelites at Jericho, we have been given a mission with instructions that can seem confusing at times.

While Israel was commanded to warn Jericho from the outside, we are commanded to go into the nations. How are we expected to do this when so much around us is evil, heartless, discouraging, and frustrating? Our battle, like the Israelites', will be fought with unconventional weapons and tactics. Our weapon is the gospel and the word of God, which Jesus Himself described in Matthew 24:14:

> *This gospel of the kingdom will be proclaimed throughout the whole world as a testimony to all nations, and then the end will come.*

Our unusual methods, meanwhile, are prayer, love, grace, mercy, forgiveness, and reconciliation. We have been commanded to love the world, even when our human instinct says we should hate it. We are called to forgive the world when our human instinct says to bring the hammer of justice. Through the gospel and our weapons of love, forgiveness, and grace, the walls of unbelief will come tumbling down. Throughout this age, as the six trumpets proclaim hope in this world to be futile, we proclaim the alternative.

At the same time, it's easy to question and be frustrated with how or why God allows some of the stuff He lets persist in this world. Do you ever wonder why God waits so long to judge the world's evil? Why does He tolerate all this madness? Do you ever wish God would just get on with that seventh trumpet already? "Sound that bad boy, Jesus! Let's go!" Revelation 6:10 expresses this yearning for justice, which can lead us to moments of impatience:

> *O Sovereign Lord, holy and true, how long before you will judge and avenge our blood on those who dwell on the earth?*

After all, it's frustrating to watch wickedness thrive, especially when it begins to impact you directly. Sometimes, it can feel like we as followers of Jesus have no chance of success against the fortresses of evil. We want Him to come back and settle things, the sooner the better.

But, what if there hadn't been six trumpets warning you, exposing the truth that this world isn't worthy of your hope? What if He had chosen to blast the seventh trumpet before you were even born or had a chance to join the people of God? What if right after His resurrection, Jesus went straight to the seventh trumpet and you never had a chance to repent? What if He didn't delay that seventh trumpet long enough for you to hear the invitation to join His people and follow Him? Second Peter 3:9 reminds us God's loving patience is behind His timing:

> *The Lord is not slow to fulfill his promise as some count slowness, but is patient toward you, not wishing that any should perish but that all should reach repentance.*

It's God's kindness toward you that provided this time in history for your repentance and redemption. Thankfully, our Jesus is far more merciful and patient than we are, so He has given humanity one final chance! This world is full of Jerichos—fortresses of unbelief, pride, evil, and human wisdom in which people put all their hope. Sometimes, humankind builds beautiful, impressive, shiny walls, and for a moment we might be distracted by them, too. It's the trumpets that warn us of their collapse, exposing how foolish it is to trust in the Jerichos of this world. Followers of Jesus can hear the blare of those trumpets warning of the fate of every Jericho ever built. The six trumpets of our current age remind us, one day our Jesus will return with His seventh trumpet—and that's the day these worldly walls are coming down!

Can you hear the trumpets of God's word warning us of His coming judgment? Do you see how they reveal the hopeless mess this world has made of itself? As these trumpets expose this world's failure and inability to keep its promises, they drive you toward the gospel. That's God's grace! The first six trumpets are playing a song of mercy. Let them be a reminder to you that there's no hope inside Jericho. Join the people outside the city, who follow their commander, the Lamb, wherever He goes.

Go into the Land!

CHAPTER TEN

Joy on Judgment Day
(Joshua 6:15-27)

Coaching high school football was a huge part of my life and ministry for twenty-five years. It was an identity, a job, and a fraternity I loved. In the summer of 1985, I was seventeen and had just graduated. I was coaching JV punt return and kickoff return, the lowest rung of coaching. Somehow, I got invited to an exclusive coach's clinic run by my childhood hero, Coach Bobby Bowden. For three days, I was in a room with my childhood hero and the greatest high school coaching legends from throughout the state. They were teaching us valuable coaching techniques and how to coach football as followers of Jesus. I was unbelievably humbled and left speechless because I knew what was obvious to all: I didn't deserve to be there. I hadn't coached my first play, yet there I was, the only JV coach in a room with Coach Bowden and the best coaches in Florida! I was the least qualified in the room.

When we all introduced ourselves, I said, "I'm Coach Joe Davis, JV special teams at Temple Heights Christian School." Right after that, our head coach, who had known me since ninth grade, said, "I'm glad to be here with Coach Joey." I always hated my childhood nickname, Joey. But that day, I didn't care. I was so filled with humble gratitude to be among these coaching legends and godly men—I couldn't have cared less what they called me!

Rahab and her family must have had a similar feeling, but much more intense, on Jericho's judgment day. Joshua 6:15–17 sets the scene:

> *On the seventh day they rose early, at the dawn of day, and marched around the city in the same manner seven times. It was only that day that they marched around the city seven times. ^{16} And at the seventh time, when the priests had blown the trumpets, Joshua said to the people, "Shout, for the* LORD *has given you the city. ^{17} And the city and all that is within it shall be devoted to the* LORD *for destruction. Only Rahab the prostitute and everyone in her house shall live because she hid the messengers we sent."*

History—Jericho's Judgment Day

Warnings Rejected

The people of Jericho had centuries of exposure to the God of Israel. They had seen displays of His power and heard messengers and prophets proclaim both warnings of judgment and the good news of mercy. After six final days of trumpets, the inhabitants inside the walls of Jericho were fully informed and fully warned. These warnings of judgment and invitations to mercy had been ignored for centuries and, now, for one final week.

Why would they ignore these warnings? Certainly, their spies had reported Israel's crossing of the raging Jordan River. Stories they heard about the Red Sea parting were only forty years old. The news of Israel defeating vastly superior forces of the Amorite kings in the wilderness was still fresh. How could they see all this evidence but still reject God's invitation? Like many today, Jericho resented God so much and loved this world so much that nothing would pry them away from Jericho.

Catastrophic Consequences

Jericho knew Israel's invasion was coming, but they would be surprised by the severity of their judgment afterward. Paul's admonition to the hard-hearted in Romans 2:5 could have applied to the people of Jericho:

> *Because of your hard and impenitent heart, you are storing up wrath for yourself on the day of wrath when God's righteous judgment will be revealed.*

The norm after the conquest of ancient cities was to capture any valuable resources rather than destroy them. This could include people for forced labor, goods for spoils of war, livestock, precious metals, and buildings or structures. In addition, the women of conquered cities were taken as concubines by the conquerors, serving multiple purposes: to humiliate the defeated, infiltrate their bloodline, increase the population of the conquerors, and force assimilation.

All this sounds bad, but it was their baseline expectation in those days. The people of Jericho were willing to risk living that way. They assumed the Israelites, if victorious, would take the normal actions, plundering the city and enslaving its inhabitants. The chance to continue some semblance of the life they had in Jericho was worth living under the rule of the Israelites. But, that wouldn't happen, as Joshua made clear in verses 18 to 21:

> *"But you, keep yourselves from the things devoted to destruction, lest . . . you take any of the devoted things and make the camp of Israel a thing for destruction and bring trouble upon it. [19] But all silver and gold, and every vessel of bronze and iron, are holy to the* LORD*; they shall go into the treasury of the* LORD*." [20] As soon as the people heard the sound of the trumpet, the people shouted a great shout, and the wall fell down flat, so that the people went up into the city, every man straight before him, and they captured the city. [21] Then they*

devoted all in the city to destruction; both men and women, young and old, oxen, sheep, and donkeys, with the edge of the sword.

God commanded Israel to kill everyone inside Jericho. (We'll deal with this troubling idea soon.) Yet, within this tragic story of stubbornness and total judgment is a story of mercy connecting it directly to the New Testament. One family, led by Rahab the prostitute, escaped judgment despite living a life immersed in Jericho's debauchery. Joshua 6:22–27 describes their rescue:

> *But to the two men who had spied out the land, Joshua said, "Go into the prostitute's house and bring out the woman and all who belong to her, as you swore to her." ²³ So the young men who had been spies went in and brought out Rahab and her father and mother and brothers and all who belonged to her. And they brought all her relatives and put them outside the camp of Israel. ²⁴ And they burned the city with fire, and everything in it. Only the silver and gold, and the vessels of bronze and iron, they put into the treasury of the house of the* LORD. *²⁵ But Rahab the prostitute and her father's household and all who belonged to her, Joshua saved alive. And she has lived in Israel to this day, because she hid the messengers whom Joshua sent to spy out Jericho.*
>
> *²⁶ Joshua laid an oath on them at that time, saying, "Cursed before the* LORD *be the man who rises up and rebuilds this city, Jericho. At the cost of his firstborn shall he lay its foundation, and at the cost of his*

*youngest son shall he set up its gates." *²⁷* So the LORD was with Joshua, and his fame was in all the land.*

THEOLOGY—TWO SIDES OF JUDGMENT DAY

Once again, the theology in the story of Jericho is connected directly to Revelation. Three undeniable links appear in Revelation 11:15–19:

> *Then the seventh angel blew his trumpet, and there were loud voices in heaven, saying, "The kingdom of the world has become the kingdom of our Lord and of his Christ, and he shall reign forever and ever."* ...
>
> *[18] The nations raged, but your wrath came, and the time for the dead to be judged, and for rewarding your servants, the prophets and saints, and those who fear your name, both small and great, and for destroying the destroyers of the earth."*
>
> *[19] Then God's temple in heaven was opened, and the ark of his covenant was seen within his temple. There were flashes of lightning, rumblings, peals of thunder, an earthquake, and heavy hail.*

The Seventh Trumpet

The first link is obvious: this seventh trumpet is no longer a warning. It signals final judgment, when God acts and destroys evil. The seventh trumpet in Joshua came on the day the walls collapsed in futility, exposing the wickedness inside the city. Their foolish hopes were dashed; their immense wickedness was held to account, and they were obliterated. The day Jesus returns with the seventh trumpet is the same type of event but on an exponentially grander scale. The seventh trumpet in Revelation signals judgment not just for one city but for all the unredeemed on the earth.

The People Shout!

At the seventh trumpet, in both Joshua and Revelation, we see the people of God shouting. We don't know exactly what they shouted at Jericho, but it was probably a mighty shout of faith, triumph, and victory in God's name. Revelation 11:15, however, has told us exactly what the people of God, those who follow the Lamb, will shout on that day: "The kingdom of the world has become the kingdom of our Lord and of his Christ, and he shall reign forever and ever." I can imagine the Israelites likewise proclaiming the arrival of God's presence symbolized by the ark, and His authority over the promised land, as Jericho's walls crumbled.

The Ark (God's Presence)

The ark of the covenant was at Jericho on the seventh day of trumpets. It appears in Revelation, too, when the seventh trumpet heralds Jesus' earthly kingdom. God's presence in both places on both days is a beautiful connection between the Old and New Testaments and also points to Jesus, as God's presence with us.

Now, the story of Jericho ends with a dire warning for anyone who wishes to rebuild the walls of Jericho. Whoever might try to rebuild the fortress of Jericho would be cursed, losing their firstborn son and their youngest son. Indeed, under King Ahab, one of the leaders in Israel later tried to rebuild Jericho and paid that very price, according to 1 Kings 16:34:

> *In his days [Ahab's reign] Hiel of Bethel built Jericho. He laid its foundation at the cost of Abiram his firstborn and set up its gates at the cost of his youngest son Segub, according to the word of the LORD, which he spoke by Joshua son of Nun.*

But, why would someone want to rebuild Jericho, literally or figuratively? Perhaps they don't believe God will keep His promises. Maybe they love this world more than God's grace or don't understand their own depravity. Perhaps they have no joy and refuse to be supernaturally satisfied with the presence of God over anything else. This warning was a stark reminder: once you leave Jericho and become part of God's covenant, never go back! There are consequences to abandoning His presence.

Personal—
Humble Gratitude on Judgment Day

Through God's grace, a shameful past becomes inspiration for gratitude, worship, and hope. Do you think Rahab ever would have been tempted to rebuild Jericho? No. She was fully satisfied among God's people. By faith, Rahab made the difficult choice to move on from Jericho to a new identity as a child of God's covenant with Israel. By His grace, Rahab and her entire family now numbered among God's people! It was something none of them deserved.

Imagine the relief, the immense gratitude, and the joy they felt on that seventh day of trumpets. What were their thoughts as they saw Jericho's walls, once their hope, fall and judgment overwhelm the city. Can you see how God did for them the same thing He did for you when He called you out into His light? In Paul's words in Colossians 1:13–14:

> *He has delivered us from the domain of darkness and transferred us to the kingdom of his beloved Son, [14] in whom we have redemption, the forgiveness of sins.*

Rahab's experience on that day foreshadowed what we will experience on the day Jesus returns with His seventh trumpet. As much as Rahab was filled with amazement, joy, and gratitude, imagine what we will feel on the day of the Lord. We'll be awestruck, grateful, and stunned that we have been counted among those God has chosen to redeem!

But, if God redeemed Rahab and brought her into His people, why was she referred to as "the prostitute" even after that day? I don't think any of us would care to have that nickname. Yet, many centuries later, in the New Testament, she was still known as "Rahab the prostitute." Take the record of her story in Hebrews 11:30–31, for example:

> *By faith, the walls of Jericho fell down after they had been encircled for seven days. [31] By faith Rahab the prostitute did not perish with those who were*

disobedient, because she had given a friendly welcome to the spies.

She was one of God's people; she was no longer a prostitute. So, why call her that? It would be like you giving me a nickname from my past failures or weaknesses: "Pastor Joe the ice cream addict," "Pastor Joe who was fired by three churches," "Pastor Joe the control freak," "Pastor Joe with ADD," or "Pastor Joe with US41 road rage." When Rahab saw this nickname in writing, do you think she got upset? Frustrated? "I'm not that person anymore!"

Perhaps she had a different reaction. Maybe she raised her hand in agreement and humble worship through tears of joy: "Yes! That was me! My old life represented everything Jericho stood for. I deserved to be inside the walls that day, because I didn't know God. I had no connection to His people. All my hope was in Jericho, its lifestyle, its people, and its walls. I deserved to be judged just like the rest of Jericho, but by God's grace and through the gift of faith, I've been redeemed!" First Corinthians 6:11 reminds followers of Jesus that we've all gone through some version of this redemption experience:

> *And such were some of you. But you were washed, you were sanctified, you were justified in the name of the Lord Jesus Christ and by the Spirit of our God.*

God didn't snatch Rahab out of Jericho because Israel needed more prostitutes. It was to transform her. His grace sets you free from pretending to be something you aren't and provides gratitude for what Jesus has done. We don't hide what we used to be, because by God's sovereign grace, the gospel has set us free from shame.

Imagine the day of judgment when you, like Rahab, find yourself numbered among those who follow the Lamb. On that day, you won't be ashamed of who you were before Jesus redeemed you and transformed your heart and life. And in your joy, just like Israel around Jericho, you will join the rest of God's people in shouting the words of Revelation 11:18: "The nations raged, but your wrath came, and the time for the dead to be judged, and for rewarding your servants, the prophets and saints, and those who fear your name, both small and great, and for destroying the destroyers of the earth."

Like Rahab, we'll all be fully aware that none of us deserve to be there; we will all be full of joy Jesus has redeemed us! Just like Coach Joey at that coach's clinic and Rahab the prostitute from Jericho, we won't care what people have said about us. The only thing that will matter is how Jesus has used the warnings of the gospel to snatch us out of Jericho.

Even now, Rahab's redemption story ought to fill us with supernatural satisfaction with the presence of God over anything Jericho could ever offer us. Let's be glad to be numbered among the people of God!

CHAPTER ELEVEN

Achan's Sin: God's Correction
(Joshua 7)

Have you ever heard someone say that if you are disobedient, God will withhold His blessings or withdraw His protection? As followers of Jesus, we never want to be outside of God's blessing and protection; it's a scary prospect. Is God a punitive, distant judge who withdraws His presence from His people when they step out of line? How can we know if our sin is so bad we're entering that danger zone?

Maybe you've felt that way before, like God was withholding blessings and protection because of your sinful choices. Many people see the story of Achan the Israelite as an example of how God will punish His children when they sin by letting them suffer. But, what if I told you God never withholds His blessing and protection from His chosen people no matter what we do? What if I told you thinking that way reveals a lack of understanding of what God's grace is all about? What you interpret as God withholding His blessing or protection may be the complete opposite.

The story of Achan is intended to be an encouragement and reassurance God keeps His promises to His people, but many of the details are disturbing and sad. The trouble began with the Israelites' hasty attack on the city of Ai, recounted in Joshua 7:1–6:

> *But the people of Israel broke faith regarding the devoted things, for Achan ... of the tribe of Judah took some of the devoted things. And the anger of the LORD burned against the people of Israel.*
>
> *² Joshua sent men from Jericho to Ai, which is near Beth-aven, east of Bethel, and said to them, "Go up and spy out the land." The men spied out Ai. ³ And they returned to Joshua and said to him, "Do not have all the people go up, but let about two to three thousand men to attack Ai. Do not make the whole people toil up there, for they are few." ⁴ So about three thousand men went up there from the people. And they fled before the men of Ai, ⁵ and the men of Ai killed about thirty-six of their men and chased them before the gate as far as Shebarim and struck them at the descent. The hearts of the people melted and became as water.*
>
> *⁶ Then Joshua and the elders of Israel tore their clothes and fell on their faces before the ark of the LORD until the evening. And they put dust on their heads.*

HISTORY—SPIRITUAL OVERCONFIDENCE

Pitiful Ai

After the crossing of the Jordan and the victory at Jericho, the Israelites were brimming with confidence and national pride. They saw themselves as being on God's side, the side of righteousness. They also had a powerful army with successes under their belt. Yes, God brought the walls down, but they went into the city and obliterated Jericho's army in hand-to-hand combat. Joshua and Israel were energized and ready for the next challenge: the tiny, under-fortified outpost called Ai, ten miles north of Jericho.

Like a truck stop on the highway, Ai sat on the road between Jericho and Bethel. As the battle of Jericho was winding down, Joshua did the logical thing: he sent spies to Ai. These scouts reported that Ai, which relied on the fortress city of Jericho as a shield from invading armies, wasn't well defended. They recommended to Joshua that only 3,000 troops would be needed to overrun Ai, about 0.5 percent of the 600,000 Israelites. This was solid military strategy—minimizing the massive logistics required to relocate and deploy 600,000 troops. The smaller the fighting force, the less food, weapons, supplies, and livestock you needed for each day on the battlefield. This all seems like wise planning, but there was something missing in Israel's plans for Ai, compared to Jericho: reliance on God.

Embarrassing Failure

Have you ever felt certain you knew what God wanted and were shocked when it didn't happen? That's what happened at Ai. Joshua and Israel expected an easy victory: "If God made Jericho's walls fall, this will be a piece of cake!" Based on the incredible success they'd just experienced, certainly Israel should be able to overrun this little roadside outpost easily. Ai would be no match for the people of God! But, Joshua didn't know there was a secret cancer brewing in the camp.

A handful of soldiers at Ai turned the attackers back; they fled downhill in fear, losing thirty-six men. The Israelites were stunned; Joshua was devastated. Joshua 7:7–13 describes his conversation with God in the aftermath of this defeat:

> *Joshua said, "Alas, O Lord GOD, why have you brought us over the Jordan at all, to give us into the hands of the Amorites, to destroy us? Would that we had been content to dwell beyond the Jordan!* [8] *O Lord, what can I say, when Israel has turned their backs before their enemies!* [9] *For the Canaanites and all the inhabitants of the land will hear of it and will surround us and cut off our name from the earth. And what will you do for your great name?"*
>
> [10] *The LORD said to Joshua, "Get up! Why have you fallen on your face?* [11] *Israel has sinned; they have transgressed my covenant that I have commanded them; they have taken some of the devoted things; they*

> have stolen and lied and put them among their own belongings. ¹² Therefore the people of Israel cannot stand before their enemies. They turn their backs before their enemies, because they have become devoted for destruction. I will be with you no more, unless you destroy the devoted things from among you. ¹³ Get up! Consecrate the people and say, 'Consecrate yourselves for tomorrow; for thus says the LORD, God of Israel, "There are devoted things in your midst, O Israel. You cannot stand before enemies until you take away the devoted things from among you."'"

In other words, Joshua protested to God, "How could You let Israel be embarrassed by such a small outpost like Ai? God, why go through all this trouble to bring us across the Jordan just to be humiliated here at this chariot stop? God, isn't this embarrassing for You, too? You let Your people run in fear from Ai, defeated and embarrassed!"

But, Joshua and most of Israel didn't know, until God revealed it, that one of the Israelites had directly disobeyed God, stealing some of the things they were supposed to devote to Him. Joshua determined the man Achan was the culprit and confronted him, in Joshua 7:18–23:

> And he brought near his household man by man, and Achan the son of Carmi, son of Zabdi, son of Zerah, of the tribe of Judah, was taken. ¹⁹ Then Joshua said to Achan, "My son, give glory to the LORD God of Israel and give praise to him. And tell me now what you have done; do not hide it from me." ²⁰ And Achan answered Joshua, "Truly I have sinned against the LORD God of

> *Israel, and this is what I did:* ²¹ *when I saw among the spoil a beautiful cloak from Shinar, and 200 shekels of silver, and a bar of gold weighing 50 shekels, then I coveted them and took them. And see, they are hidden in the earth inside my tent, with the silver underneath."*
>
> ²² *So Joshua sent messengers, and they ran to the tent; and behold, it was hidden in his tent with the silver underneath.* ²³ *And they took them out of the tent and brought them to Joshua and to all the people of Israel. And they laid them down before the* LORD.

It's worth repeating that unlike at Jericho, the Israelites moved against Ai without any instructions from God. "We've got this one, God!" they thought. Perhaps Joshua, too, assumed Ai would be so easy, they didn't need Jericho-type instructions. Often, we underestimate the power of our enemy—or fail to correctly identify him in the first place. Joshua assumed all of the Israelites were equally committed to God's commands, like we may assume everyone in the church is a sincere follower of Jesus. Both assumptions are flawed.

THEOLOGY—GOD'S PROTECTION

Get Up and Grow!

In the aftermath of Ai, Joshua and Israel were discouraged, reeling, confused, and grieving. They wallowed in self-pity. I love how God responded—not with, "Oh, what's wrong, little Joshie? Are you sad? It's okay. Everything will be okay." Far from it! He answered, in effect, "Joshua, stop crying and get off the ground. Israel has a big problem here. Now, together, we are all going to fix it. It's time to get up and grow from what happened at Ai!" And so they did, in a decisive and drastic way, in Joshua 7:24–26:

> *And Joshua and all Israel with him took Achan the son of Zerah, and the silver and the cloak and the bar of gold, and his sons and daughters and his oxen and donkeys and sheep and his tent and all that he had. And they brought them up to the Valley of Achor. ²⁵ And Joshua said, "Why did you bring trouble on us? The LORD brings trouble on you today." And all Israel stoned him with stones. They burned them with fire and stoned them with stones. ²⁶ And they raised over him a great heap of stones that remains to this day. Then the LORD turned from his burning anger.*

Does this sequence of events, and the fact God allowed it, trouble you? Does He seem harsh or unfair to you, in this story? Why would God allow one person's sin to cause such widespread embarrassment? We'll dig deeper into questions about Achan's fate in the next chapter, but here's the crucial part to keep in mind: this was all Achan's fault!

Protection, Not Punishment

Many people interpret Israel's defeat at Ai as a result of God withdrawing His blessing and protection, but I see it differently. Yes, they lost thirty-six men. But, that was one percent of their entire force. From a human perspective, this incident seems like a judgment, yet I believe it's another example of God's love and grace.

Elsewhere in the Bible, even in the book of Joshua, we see what God's judgment looks like, and the setback at Ai wasn't it. God's judgment looks like Jericho in shambles, totally obliterated; it also looks like the seventh trumpet in Revelation. Divine punishment is reserved for Judgment Day. By contrast, the defeat and loss of life at Ai were God's grace, mercy, and love in action, as a father disciplines his beloved child according to Proverbs 3:11–12:

> *My son, do not despise the* LORD's *discipline or be weary of his reproof,* ¹² *for the* LORD *reproves him whom He loves, as a father the son in whom He delights.*

When you step back and look at the bigger picture, you realize the consequences could have been much more severe. Israel was in a war requiring spiritual vigilance and preparation. The task of defeating Ai paled in comparison to the larger campaign. God, in fact, was preventing further harm, stopping the spread of harmful habits among His people. I don't believe God withheld His love or protection. Instead, He was displaying it powerfully in ways Israel couldn't comprehend at first.

Imagine the ramifications if God hadn't allowed the Israelites' defeat that day and Achan's sin had gone unnoticed by Joshua. People close to Achan would have learned of his disobedience and been tempted to follow suit. How much heartache, pain, and death might have befallen Israel if this sin had been allowed to proliferate? Disobedience would have spread like a stealthy cancer through Israel, resulting in pain, suffering, and death far outweighing Ai.

God knows His people are prone to stray. In His love and care, He shepherds them back onto the right path. Through His divine wisdom, God revealed hidden evil among the Israelites before the situation got out of control.

PERSONAL—GOD'S CORRECTION

This story isn't about God's judgment, punishment for His people, or withholding blessings. On the contrary, it's showing God will never permit anything, including our own sin, to overtake His redeemed. When God corrects His children, He's not withholding His blessings and protection—He's pouring them out! The story of Ai and Achan reminds us God will take whatever means necessary to sanctify and prepare His people for the Day of the Lord. It provides another example of God expressing His profound, unconditional love for His people.

Let's be thankful God's love isn't superficial, fair-weather affection based on our religious performance. Does that sound like mercy? Mercy isn't about getting tossed a "grace biscuit" as a reward when you're good and getting swatted with a rolled-up newspaper when you're bad. That's why David said, in Psalm 119:71 and 119:75:

> *It is good for me that I was afflicted, [so] that I might learn your statutes. . . . [75] I know, O LORD, that your*

rules are righteous, and that in faithfulness you have afflicted me.

Like Joshua and Israel at Ai, do you often mistake God's loving correction as punishment or judgment? As we learned in Revelation and from what happened to Jericho, God's correction doesn't look anything like judgment. God never withholds blessings from His children! Setbacks, trials, or challenges that stem from our choices are not God's disapproval or punishment; they're His mercy at work!

Can you see God's correction as a comforting protective measure, a testament to His deep love for us? The metaphor of a shepherd in Psalm 23 comes to mind: "Thy rod and thy staff, they comfort me." His correction is a supernaturally ordained chance for honesty, prioritizing, and realignment with God's plan. His correction is not for punishment; it's always for our preservation, a blessing that brings us back into covenant with Him. Discipline does not equal wrath! God's correction is reassuring evidence of His commitment to perfecting us for the Day of the Lord. That's what Ai would become for Joshua and the Israelites, and it's what God's correction is for us, too: an act of love, guidance, and protection that reflects His deep, enduring commitment to His people.

Through the Holy Spirit, these corrections provide pivotal moments for change that otherwise would never take place. Our natural tendency is to deny, ignore, and diminish these moments rather than respond with vulnerability and teachability. But, knowing God's correction is an expression of His love, what's the best way to respond to these

Achan's Sin: God's Correction

moments? How do we maximize these blessings from a loving Father? With transparency, humility, and repentance, all in community the way Hebrews 10:24–25 teaches us:

> *And let us consider how to stir up one another to love and good works, ^{25} not neglecting to meet together, as is the habit of some, but encouraging one another, and all the more as you see the Day drawing near.*

Maximizing these teachable moments from God starts with understanding His correction is not something to be processed in isolation. His correction should be processed in community, providing us a chance to fulfill the command given in Hebrews. Isolation is what we do when we feel shame or when we want to feel sorry for ourselves or blame God. Yet, He has designed His redeemed always to be interconnected by His Spirit, including when He offers correction.

As a community, we understand the gospel sets us free from the burden of hiding sin. We learned that from Rahab's story! Vulnerability and affectionate accountability are things we celebrate and encourage, allowing us to learn how to love one another relentlessly. This is the essence of living out our faith in community.

So, what's the best way to start? What are the first steps in processing God's correction together in community? James 5:16 gives us an answer:

> *Therefore, confess your sins to one another and pray for one another, [so] that you may be healed. The prayer of a righteous person has great power as it is working.*

What's your natural reaction when sin is exposed? To ignore it? Rationalize it? Wallow in self-pity, blaming God? Do you naturally desire to confess your faults to one another or see vulnerability as a sign of spiritual strength?

Creating a culture of vulnerability and relentless love *doesn't* happen naturally; it requires supernatural intervention. Discerning God's loving correction requires spiritual wisdom. Responding to correction with vulnerability and repentance requires courage, trust, humility, and a willingness to support each other as we follow Jesus. By realizing, together, that God's loving correction is a blessing and a vital expression of His love and protection, we become willing to receive God's correction within a vulnerable, loving community. This proves we are God's people.

Remember when Jesus told us, His people, to go into the land? He promised us no matter what, He will never leave or forsake us. Seeing God as one who withdraws His presence and protection when we fail doesn't reconcile with what Jesus says. Internalizing the truth about God's correction frees us to cherish those moments rather than dread and resent them. Instead of seeing God's correction as judgment or rejection, we receive them as expressions of the Father's love.

CHAPTER TWELVE

Achan's Sin: Revealing and Removing Evil
(Joshua 7)

Have you ever wondered what it would be like if everyone knew who you really are, deep down, and God judged you for it? Do you have secret sins that might need to be exposed, sins that could have a terrible impact on your community? Maybe you've wondered how far God's patience with you will go when it comes to your sinfulness. In the story of Achan, after all, we see God's swift and harsh judgment on one disobedient man and his entire family for a secret sin. Many people see Achan's story as a sober warning about secret sins and a reminder to act right or face severe consequences.

It's true God takes evil seriously, and we learned in the story of Jericho how He deals with evil harshly and severely.

How do we reconcile God's harsh judgment of Achan with His claim He is a patient, merciful Father to His people?

Consider whether God's handling of Achan might be meant as a warning but also as a reminder of His love for His people—and His low tolerance for evil that infiltrates them. He will not allow evil to derail His grace! Joshua 7:14–18 details God's action plan for exposing the secret sin among the Israelites:

> *"In the morning therefore you shall be brought near by your tribes. And the tribe that the LORD takes by lot shall come near by clans. And the clan that the LORD takes by lot shall come near by households. And the household that the LORD takes by lot shall come near man by man. [15] And he who is taken with the devoted things shall be burned with fire, he and all that he has, because he has transgressed the covenant of the LORD, and because he has done an outrageous thing in Israel."*

> *[16] So Joshua rose early in the morning and brought Israel near tribe by tribe, and the tribe of Judah was taken. [17] And he brought near the clans of Judah, and the clan of the Zerahites was taken. And he brought near the clan of the Zerahites man by man, and Zabdi was taken. [18] And he brought near his household man by man, and Achan the son of Carmi, son of Zabdi, son of Zerah, of the tribe of Judah, was taken.*

HISTORY—EVIL EXPOSED

Achan Confronted

Once Joshua got over the self-pity brought on by the failure at Ai, he did as God commanded to find the culprit. Joshua started by walking past the tribes until God revealed the thief was from the tribe of Judah. Then Joshua walked by the families within Judah until God showed him the culprit lived among the family of Zerah. One by one, Joshua walked among the men from the clan of Zerah until finally God exposed Achan as the thief.

Now, keep in mind these people all knew each other. This revelation of disobedience was personal; it was embarrassing. Joshua started off by inviting Achan to give praise to God by confessing what he had done, in Joshua 7:19–23:

> *Then Joshua said to Achan, "My son, give glory to the LORD God of Israel and give praise to Him. Tell me now what you have done; do not hide it from me." [20] And Achan answered Joshua, "Truly I have sinned against the LORD God of Israel, and this is what I did: [21] when I saw among the spoil a beautiful cloak from Shinar, and 200 shekels of silver, and a bar of gold weighing 50 shekels, then I coveted them and took them. And see, they are buried inside my tent, with the silver underneath."*
>
> *[22] So Joshua sent messengers, and they ran to the tent; and behold, it was hidden in his tent with the silver underneath. [23] And they took them out of the tent and*

> *brought them to Joshua and to all the people of Israel. And they laid them down before the* LORD.

Achan was caught, his sin fully exposed. He had no choice but to confess what he took, why, and where it was hidden. Everything was retrieved, and Joshua took Achan, everything he owned, his livestock, and his family to the place the Israelites would call the Valley of Achor, or "Valley of Trouble."

Achan and His Family Judged

There, in the Valley of Trouble, Achan was confronted and convicted. Joshua 7:24–25, we read in the previous chapter, describes how Achan and his entire family were stoned and burned, along with all his property, stolen and otherwise. In Joshua 7:26, the Israelites left a monument, a heap of stones like they'd constructed at the Red Sea, as a reminder of how God deals with sin threatening His people:

> *They raised over him a great heap of stones that remains to this day. Then the* LORD *turned from his burning anger. Therefore, to this day the name of that place is called the Valley of Achor.*

Let's be honest—this is a troubling story of God's response to Achan's secret sin. Does the severity of the consequences for Achan make you nervous at all? It seems all he did was steal some treasures and bury them in his tent. Stealing from God is not great, but . . . his kids died for it? Why would Achan's wife, his children, and his children's wives all die along with Achan? And the cows, too? After all,

Achan was also part of God's chosen people. Wouldn't you think he would at least get a second chance after confessing his wrongdoing?

It's even more puzzling when the way God treated Achan's family is compared to the way He treated Rahab the prostitute and her family. Rahab was guilty of many sins, maybe more than Achan, but was spared the judgment Jericho suffered. By mercy and grace, this Gentile woman and her entire family were folded into the family of God's chosen people! In contrast, Achan suffered the same catastrophic total judgment as everyone inside Jericho.

Ananias and Sapphira

We can't dismiss the way God dealt with Achan as "Old Testament fire" stuff, because it reflects the way He always deals with evil. A similar story took place in the early church, in Acts 5, involving the married couple Ananias and Sapphira. The church in those days was thriving and growing, relentlessly loving one another, worshiping together, and meeting needs. Ananias and Sapphira sold a piece of property and claimed to give all of it to the church to meet the needs of the hurting among them. But, they secretly held back some of the money for themselves, and God exposed all this to Peter, who confronted them. At first, they denied it; ultimately, they were struck down on the spot. Again, stealing is not good—but man, that's harsh!

These two stories both involve lying or deceit in relation to God's community (Israel and the church, respectively).

They are not merely warnings about personal moral failures but about things that could derail the integrity of the community. In both instances, God's wrath came quickly, with no opportunity for repentance, no second chances. God is slow to anger, yet here, judgment was immediate.

THEOLOGY—GOD PROTECTS HIS PEOPLE

It's natural to be troubled by the severity of God's commands to Joshua on how to deal with Achan and his family. Like the death penalty for deceit in the case of Ananias and Sapphira, it seems harsh, appearing on the surface to be incompatible with mercy and grace. How would your history match up to Achan's or Ananias' or Sapphira's? Would God deal with you the same way? This doesn't seem like the God who loves His children, described in Psalm 103:8–10:

> The LORD is merciful and gracious, slow to anger and abounding in steadfast love. ⁹ He will not always chide, nor will He keep His anger forever. ¹⁰ He does not deal with us according to our sins, nor repay us according to our iniquities.

Clearly, God wasn't very patient with Achan, was He? He wasn't patient with Ananias and Sapphira, either. Let's not pretend this isn't concerning, but we can ask ourselves: what are we missing? How do we reconcile God's apparent lack of patience with His promises to be gracious toward His people, even when we don't deserve it? It's possible there's more going on in both stories than what we see on the surface; we need to dig deeper.

First, Achan and his family were living among the tribe of Judah, which included the line of Jesus the Messiah. Achan's children and his family would have to be judged as well as Achan himself, because God was protecting the line of Jesus!

Second, we can question the premise that when God was dealing with Achan and his family, or with Ananias and Sapphira, He was in fact dealing with His children. Scripture points to the contrary.

Like Judas Iscariot among Jesus' disciples, Ananias and Sapphira were living among God's people, but they were not His people. In fact, Peter confronted Ananias and Sapphira and asked, "Why has Satan filled your heart to lie to the Holy Spirit?" Satan had entered their hearts, like he had entered Judas's heart before he betrayed Jesus.

Paul also taught that just because you're descended from Israel, like Achan, doesn't mean you are part of the covenant God made with His people: "For no one is a Jew who is merely one outwardly, nor is circumcision outward and physical" (Romans 2:28). The same is true in the church today, where membership or weekly attendance doesn't necessarily mean you're following Jesus, who said in Matthew 7:21–23:

> *Not everyone who says to me, "Lord, Lord," will enter the kingdom of heaven, but the one who does the will of my Father who is in heaven. *[22]* On that day many will say to me, 'Lord, Lord, did we not prophesy in your name, and cast out demons in your name, and do many mighty works in your name?' *[23]* And then will I*

declare to them, "I never knew you; depart from me, you workers of lawlessness."

We live with the chilling reality that Satan strategically plants children of darkness among God's people. In Matthew 13:24–30, Jesus told a story of a farmer who plants wheat in his field, but the enemy comes at night planting weeds. It's a metaphor for how Satan constantly seeks to infiltrate God's community with evil and how God deals with such threats. At the very moment it benefits His people the most, God exposes evil, gathers it, and judges it with fire. God tolerates the presence of evil while redemption for His children unfolds, until the critical moment—the perfect time for justice—arrives.

Now, don't minimize the danger of sin and its negative impacts on us. After all, Israel lost thirty-six men at Ai because of sin. But, these stories aren't primarily warnings for God's people; they're comforting promises about our redemption. God promises not to let evil disrupt our redemption. We will not be overcome by it—of that He'll make certain.

Personal—
Patience and Protection for His People

These stories display the lengths God will go to in order to preserve His people and His plan of redemption for them. His immediate and severe judgments in these situations were really acts of divine preservation of His people, emphasizing

His determination never to allow evil to derail their redemption. The consequences of Achan's sin emphasize God's care for His covenant community and His commitment to preserving their faithfulness. Jesus is a loving shepherd who protects His flock from threats within, like Ananias and Sapphira, which we might not perceive or resist on our own. As a shepherd kills a bear or wolf, Jesus comes against evil, constantly preserving those given ears to hear His voice.

You should be comforted by how differently God deals with His people compared to Achan, Ananias, and Sapphira. They receive punishment, judgment, and condemnation, while we are promised patience, correction, and grace. They're eradicated from the community of God's people, but you are irresistibly called into community with God's people! Exodus 34:6–7 describes God's ways with those of us who are part of His family:

> ... *The* LORD, *a God merciful and gracious, slow to anger, and abounding in steadfast love and faithfulness,* [7] *keeping steadfast love for thousands, forgiving iniquity and transgression and sin...*

Throughout Scripture are examples of how God dealt differently with the sins of His children. Repeatedly through the Old Testament, God showed this patience and mercy for the people of Israel despite their repeated failures. Consider the way God dealt with the sins of Abraham and Sarah, whom He corrected but didn't kill. Or, when Moses took justice into his own hands and murdered an Egyptian soldier. What about Jonah, when he directly disobeyed God and ran from what God had called him to? He established the nation of Israel through Jacob, who had stolen his brother's birthright, and Jacob's sons, even those who sold their brother Joseph into slavery. Recall God's patience with the Israelites in the wilderness, despite their daily whining and their worship of a golden calf. The greatest kings of Israel, David and his son Solomon, accrued long lists of sins, yet God corrected David without judging him and, in 1 Kings 11, gave Solomon a reprieve for his father's sake.

When Peter denied he knew Jesus, he received correction and grace, not wrath. The thief on the cross beside Jesus was clearly guilty, yet God chose to redeem him (see Luke 23:40–43). And the church in Corinth was a mess; the sexual immorality Paul condemned in 1 Corinthians 5 seems way worse than Achan's sin! But, God was patient with the Corinthians. What about the patience God showed to those churches who received letters in chapters 2 and 3 of Revelation? Man, those followers of Jesus really struggled, yet God offered them rebuke and correction instead of stoning and burning, like Achan.

If Achan were meant to be an example of how God deals with His people, how many of us would be dead already? How many times have you been disobedient to God but didn't receive what you deserve? We are guilty of the same things God judges children of darkness for: lying, stealing, immorality, unfaithfulness, and so on.

From Abraham to the thief on the cross to sinners like you and me, God has left a trail of patient love for His children, as described in 2 Peter 3:9:

Achan's Sin: Revealing and Removing Evil

The Lord is not slow to fulfill His promise as some count slowness, but is patient toward you, not wishing that any should perish, but that all should reach repentance.

We deserve the judgment Achan and his family and Ananias and Sapphira received, but Jesus endured that judgment for us. He took our judgment upon Himself, transforming us into recipients of God's patience and love instead. That work of Jesus removes us from the group that is judged harshly and places us in the protected group. From the perspective of evil and Satan, the way God deals with us compared to children of darkness is scandalous!

But, we don't take His grace and patience for granted; children of God are not designed to comfortably tolerate sin. These stories of how God deals with evil among His people should both humble you and fill you with gratitude. Because even though we don't deserve it, God chooses to treat us much differently than Achan, Ananias, and Sapphira. This contrast between evil's judgment and God's patient mercy for you is cause for encouragement and hope! No matter how deeply evil tries to infiltrate God's people, evil will be exposed in God's timing. Not only will evil fail to derail our redemption, but we will never face the kind of judgment Achan received, either. Instead, our heavenly Father will give us undeserved patience, mercy, and grace as the Spirit of God brings us into the land.

God's justice is firm and unwavering, but for those within His covenant, He promises patience, correction, and grace. You are not like Achan, Ananias, or Sapphira, who were quickly judged and eradicated from God's people. As a follower of Jesus, you are chosen, being called lovingly into community with God's people and protected by His mercy.

CHAPTER THIRTEEN

Ai Moments
(Joshua 8:1–23)

Have you ever had times when you were confidently following Jesus, on a roll, and then suddenly suffered a personal failure? Did that moment of failure cause you to be embarrassed and discouraged, making you feel unworthy of grace? If we're honest, we've all had this experience. I know I have. The impacts range from annoying to devastating. But, for followers of Jesus, these moments are when we are most intimately connected with God and His people.

For true followers of Jesus, personal failures—let's call them "Ai moments"—are when God encourages us and equips us to better serve His kingdom. In Ai moments, true followers of Jesus never quit. They always get up, try again, learn, and keep following Jesus. Joshua had the original Ai moment, which was discouraging and devastating, yet God wouldn't allow Ai to be an excuse to quit! God used Ai to make Joshua a better leader, more reliant on God than he had ever been before.

HISTORY—JOSHUA DIDN'T QUIT

Joshua Comforted

The first attempt to take Ai was a disaster. In the aftermath, Joshua was devastated and tempted to quit. God exposed the evil of Achan and his family and eradicated it from among His people, clearing the way for success. But, Achan wasn't the only problem at Ai. Joshua had been too reliant on his own wisdom and strength. Now God reassured Joshua, as recorded in Joshua 8:1–2a:

> *And the LORD said to Joshua, "Do not fear and do not be dismayed. Take all the men with you, and arise, go up to Ai. See, I have given into your hand the king of Ai, and his people, his city, and his land. ² And you shall do to Ai and its king as you did to Jericho. Only its spoil and its livestock you shall take as plunder for yourselves.*

Joshua received the same encouragement we find throughout the book of Joshua: in short, "Do not fear; I will give you the victory." This reassurance came at a good time, don't you think? Joshua's confidence was shaken; it had been a hard few days. Have you ever experienced that kind of moment? I know I have. Things are dark, but in the midst of it, God says, "I've got you."

Joshua Instructed

God provided Joshua with a battle plan in Joshua 8:2b–9:

> *"Lay an ambush against the city behind it." ³ So Joshua and all the men arose to go up to Ai. And Joshua chose 30,000 mighty men and sent them out by night. ⁴ And he commanded them, "Behold, you shall lie in ambush against the city, behind it. Do not go very far from the city, but all of you remain ready. ⁵ And I and all the people who are with me will approach the city. And when they come out against us just as before, we shall flee before them [like before]. ⁶ And they will come out after us, until we have drawn them away from the city. For they will say, 'They are fleeing from us, just as before.' So we will flee before them. ⁷ Then you shall rise up from the ambush and seize the city, for the* Lord *your God will give it into your hand. ⁸ And as soon as you have taken the city, you shall set the city on fire. You shall do according to the word of the* Lord. *See, I have commanded you." ⁹ So Joshua sent them out. And they went to the place of ambush and lay between Bethel and Ai, to the west of Ai, but Joshua spent that night among the people.*

"Do exactly as I say," God told Joshua. And notice the difference between His orders here and His instructions back at Jericho. The ambush tactic took advantage of Ai's overconfidence stemming from their recent victory over the Israelites.

God told Joshua to stage what would appear to be another victory for Ai while setting an ambush force behind the city. Five thousand troops, including Joshua, would be the bait, and 25,000 troops hidden behind Ai would swoop in to win the day.

Yet, there was an apparent wrinkle: hearing of Ai's prior success, the nearby city of Bethel joined forces with Ai against Israel. This alliance between Ai and Bethel against Israel posed a formidable threat—but also a great opportunity.

Ai Outsmarted

The enemy saw Joshua and his 5,000-man bait force. Full of confidence, they came out of Ai to meet the Israelites, in Joshua 8:10–14:

> *Joshua arose early in the morning and mustered the people and went up, he and the elders of Israel, before the people to Ai.* ¹¹ *And all the fighting men who were with him went up and drew near before the city and encamped on the north side of Ai, with a ravine between them and Ai.* ¹² *He took about 5,000 men and set them in ambush between Bethel and Ai, to the west of the city.* ¹³ *So they stationed the forces, the main encampment that was north of the city and its rear guard west of the city. But Joshua spent that night in the valley.* ¹⁴ *And as soon as the king of Ai saw this, he and all his people, the men of the city, hurried and went out early . . . to meet Israel in battle. But he did not know that there was an ambush against him behind the city.*

Joshua and his troops staged a fearful-looking retreat toward the wilderness. Ai and Bethel's forces recklessly fell for the ruse and chased them, leaving Ai undefended. Joshua 8:15–21 recounts the ensuing battle:

> *And Joshua and all Israel pretended to be beaten before them and fled in the direction of the wilderness. ¹⁶ So all the people who were in the city were called together to pursue them, and as they pursued Joshua they were drawn away from the city. ¹⁷ Not a man was left in Ai or Bethel who did not go out after Israel. They left the city open and pursued Israel.*
>
> *¹⁸ Then the* LORD *said to Joshua, "Stretch out the javelin that is in your hand toward Ai, for I will give it into your hand." And Joshua stretched out the javelin that was in his hand toward the city. ¹⁹ And the men in the ambush rose quickly out of their place, and as soon as he had stretched out his hand, they ran and entered the city and captured it. And they hurried to set the city on fire. ²⁰ So when the men of Ai looked back, behold, the smoke of the city went up to heaven, and they had no power to flee this way or that, for the people who fled to the wilderness turned back against the pursuers. ²¹ And when Joshua and all Israel saw that the ambush had captured the city, and that the smoke of the city went up, then they turned back and struck down the men of Ai.*

Now the root of Israel's initial failure, human overconfidence, became the root of Ai's downfall. At just the right moment during the chase, enemy forces heard terrifying sounds of war behind them. Reality set in as they saw Ai overrun and set on fire by the ambushing force behind them. Then, Ai and Bethel's forces turned around to see Joshua and his retreating 5,000 troops turning to charge them. To their shock, the men of Ai and Bethel had been outsmarted and trapped. The 25,000-man ambush force sliced through Ai in pursuit of the enemy, catching all the forces of Ai and Bethel in a pincer. The battle to ensue became a bloodbath, described in Joshua 8:22–23:

> *And the others came out from the city against them, so they were in the midst of Israel, some on this side, and some on that side. And Israel struck them down, until there was left none that survived or escaped. ²³ But the king of Ai they took alive, and brought him near to Joshua.*

The shock and awe that Ai and Bethel felt foreshadows what Satan would feel at the resurrection and what will befall him on the Day of the Lord described in Revelation.

THEOLOGY—HOW GOD USES AI MOMENTS

At Ai, God did two things: He exposed and eradicated embedded evil but also prepared His people to follow Him better. God wanted Joshua to strengthen his faith and listen better because the mission God had given Israel was critical. Conquering Canaan, including Ai, wasn't just about land. God was establishing a people to bless all nations through

Jesus. As we have learned, this was all a preview of Jesus' command to us to go into the land with the gospel.

But, after the first battle at Ai, Joshua and Israel were ready to quit and return to life on the other side of the Jordan River. That's why I love what God does in this story! Essentially, God said to Joshua, "Don't be afraid. Get up and try again." James exhorted Jesus' followers to this kind of perseverance in James 1:2–4:

> *Count it all joy, my brothers, when you meet trials of various kinds, ³ for you know that the testing of your faith produces perseverance. ⁴ Let perseverance have its full effect, [so] that you may be perfect and complete, lacking in nothing.*

But, God's words to Joshua were so much more than just a pep talk. He gave Israel's leader specific, rational military strategy and direction. After Joshua's initial grief, God assured him, he would be better prepared, more reliant upon God's wisdom instead of his own. This time, the Israelites would take on Ai exactly as God commanded, with humility, submission, faith, and trust in His wisdom. Ai, the failure and the success, became a valuable lesson and reminder for Israel: don't quit; get up, learn, and try again! This was God's sovereignty on display—how everything works according to His plan, in His timing.

Peter's Ai Moment

Joshua's struggles, discouragement, and comeback at Ai remind me so much of Peter's story. Just as Joshua was overconfident in the first battle of Ai, Peter was overly self-assured of his own righteousness. He would *never* deny Jesus, he insisted. To prove his confidence, that same day he boldly and foolishly attacked Roman soldiers arresting Jesus, cutting off one man's ear (see John 18:10). And like Joshua's initial overconfidence at Ai, Peter's overconfidence led to a devastating failure. After he denied he knew Jesus three times the very same night, Peter was humiliated, grieving over his failure, just like Joshua. But, both men were visited in their failure by a patient Father, who provided them with encouragement and instruction. John 21:17–19 recalls Jesus' words to Peter after His resurrection:

> *Peter was grieved because he [Jesus] said to him the third time, "Do you love me?" and he [Peter] said to him, "Lord, you know everything; you know that I love you." He [Jesus] said to him, "Feed my sheep.* [18] *Truly, truly, I say to you, when you were young, you used to dress yourself and walk wherever you wanted, but when you are old, you will stretch out your hands, and another will dress you and carry you where you do not want to go."* [19] *(This he said to show by what kind of death he was to glorify God.) And after saying this he [Jesus] said to him, "Follow me."*

Jesus sought out Peter for that second chance, not vice versa. Peter didn't believe he deserved a second chance, but Jesus did. And just as God gave Joshua instructions for his second chance, the resurrected Jesus did the same for Peter. Joshua needed to hear, "Don't be afraid," while Peter needed to hear from Jesus, "Feed My sheep and rely upon Me." From then on, Peter understood following Jesus required reliance on God's power and wisdom more than his own.

What happened after his colossal failure? Peter, the Jesus denier, became the leader of the first-century church! God used Peter as the catalyst to build the institution God would use to feed His sheep and keep them together in community throughout the age, to this moment. To experience success, both Peter and Joshua had to endure failure, embrace second chances, and abandon their own wisdom and strength for faith in God's.

PERSONAL—YOUR AI MOMENT

These two men's stories teach us God keeps His covenant with His people even when we falter. Those are Ai moments, which God uses to better equip His people to be a blessing to all nations. He uses Ai moments to help us learn from our mistakes and to rely on His wisdom and power more than our own. If you're not a follower of Jesus, Ai moments will be your excuse to give up, abandon God's people, and go your own way. Yet, these apparent low points are opportunities to reveal true followers of Jesus through our endurance, resilience, and ability to keep going. As difficult as their Ai moments were, both Joshua and Peter became better prepared to go into the land. These was why Paul wrote in Romans 5:3–5:

> *...we rejoice in our sufferings, knowing that suffering produces endurance, ⁴ and endurance produces*

character, and character produces hope, ⁵ and hope does not put us to shame, because God's love has been poured into our hearts through the Holy Spirit who has been given to us.

The days between the first defeat and the ultimate victory were difficult, but I bet Joshua wouldn't have traded them for an easy win at the start. As devastating as Peter's Ai moment must have been in the years after, I bet it became precious to him. This theme of God using Ai moments to teach, refine, and provide second chances reveals how God's covenant works. He will always provide second chances for His chosen for restoration, instruction, encouragement, and recommitment. Can you see how we need the preparation and strengthening these Ai moments provide, as we go into the land? Hebrews 10:36 explains:

For you have need of endurance, so that when you have done the will of God you may receive what is promised.

Just as God's sovereign grace was on display during Joshua and Peter's Ai moments, so it is for us today. Jesus is using Ai moments among His people to sanctify us, equip us, and prepare us for what's coming next. Our mission in the world is treacherous. Maybe you're currently facing your own Ai moment, unsure of what to do next. Perhaps you're experiencing a crisis of faith because you're trying to follow Jesus, but you've made some mistakes that have left you discouraged, disheartened, and doubting—and that's okay! We've all been there. Ai moments are part of being human. Joshua was there, too, as was Peter. God used their Ai moments to strengthen their faith and reliance on Him, and He is using yours likewise, to equip you for what's next. Ai moments can't be an excuse to quit. Get up, listen, learn, and keep following Jesus, because eventually, Ai will fall. Paul reminded the Galatian church why we don't give up in our obedience to God, in Galatians 6:9:

So let us not grow weary of doing good, for in due season we will reap, if we do not give up.

And James' words in James 1:12 remind us of that same confident hope we share in our perseverance:

Blessed is the man who remains steadfast under trial, for when he has stood the test he will receive the crown of life, which God has promised to those who love him.

You have most likely survived Ai moments in your life. You've learned from them, you've gotten up out of the dust, and you're going into the land again. Stories like Joshua's, Peter's, and countless others' reveal who God loves: those of us who won't quit because we keep getting up and following Jesus! Followers of Jesus will always return to the battle. They never abandon God's people because of an Ai moment. Faithfully following Jesus is not judged by your Kingdom win–loss record, but by your endurance.

If you aren't in an Ai moment currently, trust me, if you follow Jesus, you will be soon. None of us is perfect as we follow Jesus' command to go into the land. Sometimes, you will try something and you'll fail. When you face your Ai moment, you might feel alone, but you're not. Like Joshua, you have God and your community alongside you. So, when Ai moments come, don't quit! Stay connected with God's people, learn, trust Him, and embrace your second chance. Grace is not just about forgiveness when you mess up; it's also how God prepares you for Kingdom work.

Follower of Jesus, when you experience an Ai moment, Scripture's message for you is the same one God gave Joshua at the beginning of this chapter: "Do not fear or be dismayed. Don't quit. A second chance is coming, and God has promised that in the end, we will have the victory."

CHAPTER FOURTEEN

Strangers at Mount Ebal
(Joshua 8:24–35)

Thirty years ago, my sister, who was serving in the military at the time, invited us to her second-born child's baptism service. The church was a small African Methodist Episcopal church on Fort Jackson, and an army chaplain was the pastor. The baptism was precious; he did an amazing job. Everyone in the church was so kind and welcoming. But let me state the obvious: there were about 150 people there, and we were the only white people in the room.

After the baptism, the worship service started, and my white family stuck out. My mom, dad, and both sisters felt awkward. (Of course, the worship style didn't make me feel uncomfortable at all, because I've always had tremendous rhythm.) Even though everyone there was loving, kind, and welcoming, our family definitely felt out of place. But, two precious ladies, seeing the awkward moment, moved next to us, smiled, took our hands, and made us feel at home! We didn't know the moves, the words, or what was coming next, but it was a powerful, humbling worship experience.

Have you ever experienced feeling like a stranger until someone came along and broke that barrier? That kind of love and acceptance, inspired by the gospel, is a humbling, powerful, transformational experience. The Israelites' bloody, fiery destruction of Ai and its people may not seem like much of an invitation. I'm sure it put the remaining Canaanite nations in an extremely uncomfortable spot. Yet, in the aftermath of Ai, we find evidence some of Israel's neighbors recognized the way God cared for His people. In turn, our loving God made certain the Israelites provided a warm home for those newcomers, overcoming the initial cultural awkwardness and welcoming them into community.

History—Israel at Worship

Total Victory Over Ai

In our previous chapter, Joshua's force of 5,000 soldiers feigned a retreat while the main Israelite force of 25,000 ambushed Ai. Then the forces of Ai and Bethel were trapped and destroyed, without survivors or prisoners, between the two parts of the Israelite army. Everyone left in the city was killed, too, men and women alike. Joshua 8:24–29 describes the Israelites' victory in grim detail:

> *When Israel had finished killing all the inhabitants of Ai in the open wilderness where they pursued them, and all of them to the very last had fallen by the edge of the sword, all Israel returned to Ai and struck it down with the edge of the sword.* ²⁵ *And all who fell that day, both men and women, were 12,000, all the people of Ai.* ²⁶ *But Joshua did not draw back his hand with which he stretched out the javelin until he had devoted all the inhabitants of Ai to destruction.* ²⁷ *Only the livestock and the spoil of that city Israel took as plunder, according to the word of the* LORD *that he commanded Joshua.* ²⁸ *So Joshua burned Ai and made it forever a heap of ruins, as it is to this day.* ²⁹ *And he hanged the king of Ai on a tree until evening. And at sunset . . . [the Israelites] took his body down from the tree and threw it at the entrance of the gate of the city and raised over it a great heap of stones, which stands there to this day.*

Altogether, 12,000 people of Ai and Bethel were killed. Israel captured the king of Ai and hanged him publicly as an expression of God's judgment. After this, Ai was burned to the ground and left in ruins as a lasting reminder of His judgment. Before sunset, the king was brought down and buried under rocks at the entrance to the city. All this happened in one day. The brutality here can be legitimately troubling to read, but later in this chapter, we'll discover why it doesn't need to be. We'll learn how God's judgment always works alongside mercy and grace, just like on the Day of the Lord in Revelation.

Worship at Ebal

In Deuteronomy 27:2–6, decades earlier, God mandated that once Israel entered the promised land, they should organize a worship service between Mount Ebal and Mount Gerizim and read the law, including its blessings and its curses, or warnings:

> *And on the day you cross over the Jordan to the land that the* LORD *your God is giving you, you shall set up large stones and plaster them with plaster.* ³ *And you shall write on them all the words of this law, when you cross over to enter the land that the* LORD *your God is giving you, a land flowing with milk and honey, as the* LORD, *the God of your fathers, has promised you.* ⁴ *And when you have crossed over the Jordan, you shall set up these stones, concerning which I command you today, on Mount Ebal, and you shall plaster them with plaster.* ⁵ *And there you shall build an altar to the* LORD *your God, an altar of stones. You shall wield no iron tool on them;* ⁶ *you shall build an altar to the* LORD *your God of uncut stones. And you shall offer burnt offerings on it to the* LORD *your God . . .*

After Ai was defeated, according to Joshua 8:30–35, Joshua led Israel to this very valley near Mount Ebal, about two miles from the city of Ai, and fulfilled God's command to Moses:

> *At that time Joshua built an altar to the* LORD, *the God of Israel, on Mount Ebal,* ³¹ *just as Moses the servant of the* LORD *had commanded the people of Israel*

in the Book of the Law of Moses, "an altar of uncut stones, on which no man has wielded an iron tool." And they offered on it burnt offerings to the LORD and sacrificed peace offerings. [32] And there, in the presence of the people of Israel, he wrote on the stones a copy of the law of Moses, which he had written. [33] All Israel, sojourner as well as native born, with their elders and officers and their judges, stood on opposite sides of the ark before the Levitical priests who carried the ark of the covenant of the LORD, half of them in front of Mount Gerizim and half of them in front of Mount Ebal, just as Moses the servant of the LORD had commanded at the first, to bless the people of Israel. [34] And afterward he read all the words of the law, the law, the blessing and the curse.... [35] There was not a word that Moses commanded that Joshua did not read before all the assembly of Israel, and the women, and the little ones, and the sojourners who lived among them.

Joshua had the Israelites build the altar the way God commanded Moses, with their hands and no tools. After the priests made burnt offerings, Joshua did what God had commanded his predecessor and wrote the Ten Commandments on the stones. Then, he read the entire Torah, in a scene hearkening back to when God wrote the original commandments on stone and Moses taught them to the Israelites. The priests carried the ark of the covenant before the people. It was a powerful national worship service there in the valley! But notice, there is an additional, powerful component to this worship service, not mentioned in Deuteronomy: there were "sojourners" there—people living among the nation of Israel from other countries in that region.

THEOLOGY—IMMIGRANTS TO THE COVENANT

Scary Choice

It surely wasn't an easy decision for these ancient "sojourners," or immigrants, to abandon their old life and join the Israelites. Ancient social society was centered on extended family and clans, so most people likely didn't dream of leaving the community they were born into. Uprooting your family to start a new life with strangers, especially a strange nomadic invading force, was probably unheard of. Abandoning extended family would have been seen as foolish, a high betrayal that came with a heavy social and financial cost. Also, the people of Canaan no doubt hated Israel and demonized them as evil barbarians who hated and slaughtered all outsiders. Considering all this, the presence of "sojourners" participating in the Israelites' national worship service was quite stunning.

By joining Israel, the sojourners had made a bold statement: "I no longer believe how my family believes. I no longer embrace their values." Their change in loyalties could have gone wrong in so many ways; I'm sure they wondered beforehand if it was all a big mistake. Considering their potential reasons *not* to leave their clans and nations to follow God and Joshua, we might wonder why there would be so many sojourners among God's people, worshiping and listening to God's law in community with the Israelites.

Welcoming Strangers

The fact Israel had welcomed these sojourners to worship at Mount Ebal is a powerful testament to God's love. It reveals how even in war, the door for strangers to become a part of God's covenant people was always open! In fact, throughout the Torah, God commanded Israel fifty times to accept all strangers wanting to join them. For instance, He declared in Leviticus 19:34:

> *You shall treat the stranger who sojourns with you as the native among you, and you shall love him as yourself, for you were strangers in the land of Egypt: I am the LORD your God.*

Throughout the Old Testament are stories of non-Hebrew and non-Jewish people coming to understand God's might and His love for His people. Recall, in Joshua 2, the story of Rahab and her family, who prior to the fall of Jericho chose to worship God. Compare the way these sojourners were embraced to how God dealt with evil planted among His people, like in the case of Achan.

Stories of all God had done for His people, from Abraham to Joseph to the Exodus, all the way to Jericho and Ai, was the Old Testament gospel. As that good news went out to surrounding nations, these sojourners wanted to be a part of it, and Israel welcomed them! These were people who saw God's works and faithfulness to Israel and, by faith, abandoned their old lives. When they did that, God's people did as they were commanded and made them full citizens of Israel.

Not Strangers to God

These sojourners worshiping at Mount Ebal are key to reconciling the harsh judgment from God with the mercy of God. Judgment on people in places like Ai and Jericho came after years of informed, unrepentant rebellion against God. The judgment of the people of Jericho, Ai, and other places didn't come without ample warning. In a foreshadowing of Revelation, those people's ruin reveals the spiritual judgment awaiting any and all who refuse to join God's covenant with His people. But, for those from other nations willing to repent and join God's people, the door to this community was wide open!

God patiently waited to judge Canaan while He was calling chosen, beloved sojourners into His covenant family. In the centuries between Abraham and Joshua, God called many sojourners with ears to hear of God's love for His people. He gave these strangers the gift of faith to hear, believe, join Israel, and become worshipers of the one true God. But, for those who witnessed all this yet foolishly refused to accept God's invitation, no excuses remained.

PERSONAL—WORSHIPING WITH STRANGERS

When God planned the worship service after Ai's defeat, decades before it happened, do you think He picked this place on purpose? It was right up the road from Jericho, between Bethel and Ai, eighteen miles from the Jordan River. This spot lay in the region where everyone saw how the hand of God, His power, and His love for Israel were not legends or myths; they were real. In this region, many non-Israelite sojourners would see God's works, hear His truth, repent, believe, and worship Him. Do you think the presence of these spiritual immigrants was a surprise to God, or do you think He knew who these outsiders were, who would choose to join His people?

Stories of sojourners joining with God's people are not exclusive to the Old Testament. Never doubt the gospel's power to transform strangers into a family united in worship! Paul said it well in Ephesians 2:19, telling Jesus' followers:

> *So then you are no longer strangers and aliens (sojourners), but you are fellow citizens with the saints and members of the household of God . . .*

This reminder echoes God's words to the Israelites in Deuteronomy 10:19:

> *Love the sojourner, therefore, for you were sojourners in the land of Egypt.*

Like Israel at Mount Ebal, the church is commanded to welcome spiritual immigrants and strangers. Jesus commands us to intentionally move over, make space, provide an open seat, and live and worship alongside others. In fact, the diversity God has created in the global church is far greater than what we see at Mount Ebal. He unites people with little in common—unique backgrounds, experiences, and histories—for a powerful, singular purpose. This precious, miraculous unity is only possible through the power of the gospel.

Every local church needs to be a community like the one on Mount Ebal, who welcomes strangers through the cross. Following Jesus requires that the doors to our covenant community be open to anyone who believes in Him. The lifestyle we embrace should be welcoming to those strangers hungry for redemption. It's crucial every community of believers reflects God's heart for every sojourner in their region who God may be calling out of darkness into life, remembering the words in 1 Peter 2:10–11:

> *Once you were not a people, but now you are God's people; once you had not received mercy, but now you have received mercy. Beloved, I urge you as sojourners and exiles to abstain from the passions of the flesh, which wage war against your soul.*

Follower of Jesus, you were once a sojourner, a spiritual immigrant who heard the story of God's love for His people. You heard the gospel, repented, and were transformed into one of God's chosen people, His royal priesthood and holy nation. Anyone who believes the gospel and wants to join your covenant community should be welcomed into God's family.

That said, not just anyone can join God's covenant community; it's reserved for those who embrace what Jesus has done. The church is centered on Jesus and what He accomplished on the cross. He is the only way to the Father.

Some churches teach that we should allow anyone to join our family no matter what they believe. We can show warm, loving hospitality to those who don't believe in Jesus as we do. However, to be fully integrated into God's covenant family, embracing the gospel is essential. We must not compromise this foundation in exchange for growth or comfort. Just like Joshua at Mount Ebal, when we proclaim the gospel, we proclaim both the blessings and the curses.

If you're a stranger to the gospel, don't be nervous! Refusing to join God's covenant family exposes you to the risk of judgment, but that's no reason to despair. Like the sojourners at Mount Ebal, even though you were once far off, He has brought you near. In fact, as God orchestrated the worship at Mount Ebal, He does the same each time His church gathers to worship together. God fills His church with people He knew before the foundation of the world! He calls us together through His Spirit each time we meet, turning strangers into a worshiping family of God. If you're a sojourner, stranger, or spiritual immigrant, here's the invitation: through the gospel, Jesus is calling you to leave your old life, join His royal priesthood, and become part of the chosen nation of God's people. If you can hear that call, there is room for you to worship together with His followers, and we welcome you wholeheartedly.

CHAPTER FIFTEEN

Grace for Gibeonites: Redeemed Despite Ourselves
(Joshua 9)

When you first came to God, other than desperately wanting mercy and forgiveness, did you know what you were doing? Did you immediately display perfect repentance? Did you know exactly how to pray, what to do, and where to go?

The church is a place where newcomers turn for guidance. However, sometimes even those who should know better come to God in the wrong way. It's a result of long-time followers of Jesus who also approach God for the wrong reasons. We begin to look for ways to work the system, to get on God's good side in hopes He'll grant us selfish "blessings." We might even abuse prayer, asking for things like personal vengeance or political retribution. We should know better!

Given the ignorance of newcomers and the flawed nature of the church responsible for teaching new followers about Jesus, it's rational to ask the question: how does anyone have a chance to find God, come to Jesus, and learn to follow Him? Yet, despite all these imperfections, God's grace intervenes, overcomes, and weaves our flaws into His story of redemption.

HISTORY—FRIGHTENED KINGS

Word Spread

From the mountains to the coasts, news spread about the military victories won by Joshua and the Israelites, Joshua 9:1–2 tells us:

> *As soon as all the kings who were beyond the Jordan in the hill country and in the lowland all along the coast … heard of this, ² they gathered together as one to fight against Joshua and Israel.*

The destruction of powerful Amorite kings east of the Jordan, the fall of Jericho, and the defeat of the forces of Ai and Bethel terrified all the kings in Canaan. They were especially fearful of the miraculous power of God that was with Israel. More than fearing Israel's mighty fighting men, they feared what God had done for them at the Jordan River, Jericho, and Ai. Instead of letting fear lead them to repentance, these kings formed an alliance, choosing war over worship. They had seen God's power and knew Israel could fight, but stubbornly, they chose to fight God rather than worship Him. This is always the response of those without faith or ears to hear when the gospel is preached—stubborn, foolish refusal.

Gibeonite Desperation

Meanwhile, the Gibeonites, knowing they couldn't defeat Israel or resist God, created a ruse to manipulate Israel into a treaty. Joshua 9:3–14 explains how the people of Gibeon carried out their deception:

> *But when the inhabitants of Gibeon heard what Joshua had done to Jericho and to Ai, ⁴ they on their part acted with cunning and went and made ready provisions and took worn-out sacks for their donkeys, and wineskins, worn-out and torn and mended, ⁵ with worn-out, patched sandals on their feet and worn-out clothes. And all their provisions were dry and crumbly. ⁶ And they went to Joshua in the camp at Gilgal and said to him and to the men of Israel, "We have come from a distant country, so now make a covenant with us." ⁷ But the men of Israel said to the Hivites [of Gibeon], "Perhaps you live among us [as Canaanites we are commanded to conquer]; then how can we make a covenant with you?" ⁸ They [the Gibeonites] said to Joshua, "We are your servants." And Joshua said to them, "Who are you? Where do you come from?" ⁹ They said to him, "From a very distant country your servants have come, because of the name of the* LORD *your God. For we have heard a report of him, and all that he did in Egypt, ¹⁰ and all that he did to the two*

> *kings of the Amorites who were beyond the Jordan.... ¹¹ So our elders and all the inhabitants of our country said, 'Take provisions in your hand for the journey and go to meet them and say to them, "We are your servants. Come now, make a covenant with us."' ¹² Here is our bread. It was still warm when we took it from our houses.... ¹³ These wineskins were new when we filled them, and behold, they have burst. These garments and sandals are worn out from the very long journey." ¹⁴ So the men [of Israel] took some of their provisions but did not ask counsel from the LORD.*

Unlike Achan's deceit, in which he tried to hide his greed, the Gibeonite deception was motivated by fear of God's power and judgment. No doubt, the Gibeonites had heard how God commanded Israel to accept strangers who desired to worship God—which is why this story follows Rahab and the story of sojourners worshiping with Israel on Mount Ebal. The Gibeonites sent representatives disguised as weary travelers from far away, with worn-out clothing and stale provisions. They claimed to have traveled for months, inspired by stories about God's power. They wanted mercy and to be a part of it. They presented themselves as weary sojourners who desired to worship God. In fact, the only part of the story that was false was their claim of being from far away; the rest was true.

But, Joshua and the elders swallowed the strangers' tale whole. Without consulting God, they made a covenant with the Gibeonites, treating them with hospitality, love, and kindness, just as they had Rahab and the sojourners at Mount Ebal.

Deception Uncovered

Soon after the treaty, the Israelites discovered the Gibeonites were from nearby cities, about ten miles from Ai. Joshua 9:15–27 describes the Israelites' reactions and the fate of the Gibeonites:

> *And Joshua made peace with them and made a covenant with them, to let them live, and the leaders of the congregation [the elders] swore to them.*
>
> *[16] At the end of three days after they had made a covenant with them, they heard that they were their neighbors and that they lived among them [nearby]. [17] And the people of Israel set out and reached their cities on the third day.... [18] But the people of Israel did not attack them, because the leaders of the congregation had sworn to them by the LORD. Then all the congregation murmured against the leaders. [19] But all the leaders said to all the congregation, "We have sworn to them by the LORD, the God of Israel; and now we may not touch them. [20] This we will do to them: let them live, lest wrath be upon us, because of the oath that we swore to them." [21] And the leaders said to them, "Let them live." So they became cutters of wood and drawers of water for all the congregation, just as the leaders had said of them.*

> ²²*Joshua summoned them, and he said to them, "Why did you deceive us, saying 'We are very far from you,' when you dwell among us?* ²³ *Now therefore you are cursed, and some of you shall never be anything but servants, cutters of wood and drawers of water for the house of my God."* ²⁴ *They answered Joshua, "Because it was told to your servants for a certainty that the* LORD *your God had commanded His servant Moses to give you all the land and to destroy all the inhabitants of the land from before you—so we feared greatly for our lives because of you and did this thing.* ²⁵ *And now, behold, we are in your hand. Whatever seems good and right to do in your sight to do to us, do it."* ²⁶ *So he ... delivered them out of the hand of the people of Israel, and they did not kill them.* ²⁷ *But Joshua made them that day cutters of wood and drawers of water for the congregation and for the altar of the* LORD, *to this day...*

The people of Israel were angry at the newcomers and mad at their leaders, and they wanted the Gibeonites killed for their deception! But, Joshua and the elders felt bound to honor the treaty made in the name of God's command to receive strangers. They were instructed to be an open nation, welcoming sojourners. This command always superseded the command to destroy enemies who refused to repent. Breaking a treaty, even one made under false pretenses, would damage Israel's testimony among the surrounding nations. Confronted with their deception, the Gibeonites gladly agreed to become servants, performing two menial but critical tasks: the men became timber workers and loggers, and the women became water carriers for the people and the temple.

THEOLOGY—DIVINE PURPOSE PREVAILS

Human Wisdom

The Gibeonites believed in God. They knew His promises to Israel were true and feared not being part of them. They understood and believed in God's authority and power, which was why they pursued a treaty with Israel. The Gibeonites seemed to be repenting—maybe not elegantly, and motivated by fear, but they didn't know any better. They had never been taught about the mercy and grace part of God's covenant with His people. Ignorance forced them to rely on human wisdom.

Joshua and the elders also relied on human wisdom. They knew something was off and should have sought God's guidance first. They missed a chance to teach the Gibeonites about God's mercy. Tragically, instead of teaching them, they took advantage of their fear and manipulated them into becoming slaves. Both Israel and the Gibeonites committed the same error: faith in human wisdom over God's wisdom. Yet, who bears more responsibility for this tragedy, the Gibeonites or the Israelites?

God's Purpose

Sometimes, the Old Testament is written in a way that tells us what happens without explaining why it's important.

But, there's a powerful theological truth here: God's plan for the Gibeonites could not be derailed by human deficiency. This story follows the one about strangers and sojourners worshiping with Israel on Mount Ebal for a reason. Every circumstance worked against the Gibeonites becoming part of God's covenant with Israel, yet we know from Romans 8:28:

> *... for those who love God all things work together for good for those who are called according to his purpose.*

Humanly speaking, the Gibeonites should have faced the same fate as the people of Jericho, Ai, and many others. Did you know King Saul, inspired by evil, hated the Gibeonites so much he tried to have them all killed? (2 Samuel 21). That story proves Satan feared the crucial role the Gibeonites would play in God's plan of redemption.

Despite Israel's failure and the Gibeonites' fear and deception, God transformed them into crucial people in Israel's history. When Solomon built the temple, there is compelling evidence they played a vital part in cutting and processing all the wood. The Gibeonites became much more than lumberjacks and water carriers; they took on critical roles to support the temple. They became known as the Nethinim, or "dedicated ones," taking pride in their temple service. Even during Israel's dark time in the Babylonian Exile, the Nethinim remained dedicated in service to the people of Israel. After the Babylonian Exile, Gibeonites were listed among those returning to rebuild Jerusalem's walls and the temple.

PERSONAL—AREN'T WE ALL GIBEONITES?

The path of the Gibeonites coming to God through their deception and Israel's failure wasn't ideal. But, even when God's people do everything wrong, God's grace will always succeed in making it right. Despite their dysfunctional history with God and His people, God wouldn't allow any of it to derail His plan for them. Imagine a scenario where Israel handled this the right way and consulted God. What if Israel had responded to the initial Gibeonite deception brought on by ignorance with wisdom, love, and truth? What if Joshua and Israel, in their initial suspicion, had sought God's wisdom about how to handle the Gibeonites?

Would God have told Joshua to kill them all, like He did at Jericho? Or, do you think God might have said, "Listen, they aren't like the people of Jericho. They believe I am the one true God. They know of My wrath, but they don't know about My grace, mercy, love, and patience. Joshua, they're petrified! Tell them we know exactly who they are, and they don't need to be afraid, because I have led them to this place. There's no need to sneak or manipulate their way into My covenant family. They're welcome. Just repent and believe! Let Rahab the prostitute teach them how, by faith, she had nothing to fear when she chose to join My people. Let her teach them what it feels like to be an outsider who was welcomed, transformed, and made a part of My family. Introduce them to the sojourners at Mount Ebal, who by faith left their homes to become worshipers with you. Teach them about My unconditional love for My people, how I will never leave them or forsake them."

The Gibeonites are a case study in how God works through His people to call His chosen despite us or them. No matter what, God's grace always meets His chosen wherever they are and brings them to where He wants them to be, according to Isaiah 56:8:

> *The Lord GOD, who gathers the outcasts of Israel, declares, "I will gather yet others to him besides those already gathered."*

Over time, God wove the Gibeonites into His plan of redemption, just as He weaves each of us into it, flaws and all. God knows the heart, circumstances, and motivation of every individual. His justice is unwavering, but His mercy is vast. When you first came to God, did you do it perfectly? Did you fully understand God's mercy, His grace, and the gospel? Did you pray the perfect prayer, display perfect repentance, and integrate perfectly with the people of God on the first try? Did you immediately see who God is with absolute clarity, dispelling all the wrong ideas you had about Him and His word? Or did God's grace save you despite your flawed approach? I bet He still transforming how you approach Him to this day.

One of the best things about being part of the church is watching God gather all of us—a church full of formerly tarnished, sneaky Gibeonites, a family made of people who came to God in all the wrong ways. We've come on pathways that, humanly speaking, should never have brought us into God's covenant family. Not only that, but by the same grace and mercy, He also overcomes the flaws in the church, working through us anyway. After all, newcomers to Jesus aren't the only ones who make mistakes; long-time followers of Jesus make them, too! Yet, God works through all that, making us conduits for His gospel of grace and saving newcomers, despite us! In the process, He transforms each Gibeonite into an indispensable part of the church family we couldn't live without.

Maybe you are like the Gibeonites—brand new to following Jesus, not sure what to do or how to do it. You know God is real; you know you desperately need His mercy; but, you're afraid you don't know what to do next. That's okay! You're welcome among God's people. In fact, we are just as nervous about what God has called us to do as you are. What we don't know, we will learn together as God weaves all of us Gibeonites together into His plan of redemption.

CHAPTER SIXTEEN

Grace for Gibeonites: Who Can Stand Against Us?
(Joshua 10:1–15)

Does it seem sometimes like every element in our culture is forming an alliance to oppose what God is doing for His people? The world's view of Christianity ranges from skepticism to disdain, from mild annoyance to full-scale hate and resentment. Its opposition to the gospel runs the gamut from rude dismissal to coming after God's word with an evil alliance of vitriolic opposition. Paul described worldly opposition to Jesus' followers this way, in 2 Corinthians 4:8–9 and 4:11:

> *We are afflicted in every way, but not crushed; perplexed, but not driven to despair;* ⁹ *persecuted, but not*

*forsaken; struck down, but not destroyed.... *¹¹* For we who live are always being given over to death for Jesus' sake, so that the life of Jesus also may be manifested in our mortal flesh.*

I know I've felt like that, "pressed on every side." True followers of Jesus will never give up, but we can sure feel like quitting sometimes. So, how are we supposed to carry on? What should we do when evil is constantly swarming around us? How do we respond when the growing threat of evil and injustice around us is so great that there's no stopping it? The Gibeonites likely asked themselves similar questions shortly after they aligned with God's people, as described in Joshua chapters 9 and 10.

HISTORY—AN EVIL COALITION

Gibeon's Powerful Status

Gibeon was one of the most powerful cities in the region, with strong military capabilities. With the Israelite threat building, and Gibeon defecting to their side, the panicked kings of neighboring nations formed a powerful new alliance, described in Joshua 10:1–5:

As soon as Adoni-Zedek, king of Jerusalem, heard how Joshua had captured Ai and had devoted it to destruction, doing to Ai and its king as he had done to Jericho and its king, and how the inhabitants of Gibeon had made peace with Israel and were among them, ² he feared greatly, because Gibeon was a great city, like one of the royal cities, and because it was greater than Ai, and all its men were warriors. ³ So Adoni-zedek king of Jerusalem sent to Hoham king of Hebron, to Piram king of Jarmuth, to Japhia king of Lachish, and to Debir king of Eglon, saying, ⁴ "Come up to me and help me, and let us strike Gibeon. For it has made peace with Joshua and the people of Israel." ⁵ Then the five kings of the Amorites . . . gathered their forces and went up with all their armies against Gibeon and made war against it.

These allied kings, led by King Adoni-Zedek of what later became the city of Jerusalem, had counted on Gibeon joining them, so the news of Gibeon's treaty with Joshua and Israel was both troubling and infuriating. They saw the Gibeonite covenant with Israel as a deep betrayal and wanted to send a message with their retribution. Fueled by fear and rage at the Gibeonites for joining with the Israelites, they surrounded the city of Gibeon, intending to kill everyone. The Gibeonites knew they had no chance against this formidable alliance; without help, evil would destroy them.

Gibeon's Plea for Help

The Gibeonites sent word to Joshua, asking Israel to come to their rescue. This was a huge ask, because humanly speaking, Israel didn't have a force large enough to fight the enemy alliance. But, God assured Joshua He would fight for Israel and for Gibeon. Joshua 10:6–9 recounts the lead-up to the battle:

> *And the men of Gibeon sent to Joshua at the camp in Gilgal, saying, "Do not relax your hand from your servants. Come up to us quickly and save us and help us, for all the kings of the Amorites who dwell in the hill country are gathered against us."* ⁷ *So Joshua went up from Gilgal, he and all the people of war with him, and all the mighty men of valor.* ⁸ *And the* LORD *said to Joshua, "Do not fear them, for I have given them into your hands. Not a man of them shall stand before you."* ⁹ *So Joshua came upon them suddenly, having marched up all night from Gilgal.*

Joshua marched his entire army through the night to Gibeon. From the moment they arrived, God was active in the fight. In dramatic fashion, just in time, Israel descended from the hilltops to Gibeon to rescue its people from evil. The enemy never expected Joshua to arrive so swiftly, navigating rivers and hills in the dead of night. They were totally surprised! And so, the fighting commenced, in Joshua 10:10:

> *And the* LORD *threw them into a panic before Israel, who struck them with a great blow at Gibeon and chased them by the way of the ascent of Beth-horon and struck them as far as Azekah and Makkedah.*

God used the surprise arrival of Israel's forces to cause panic, confusion, and disorganization among the alliance. As this evil alliance heard and saw Israel coming, fear filled them, and they were defeated before the fight began! They were routed on the outskirts of Gibeon and fled down the hillsides toward the coast with the Israelites in hot pursuit. As the enemy retreated in fear, God sent a deadly hailstorm, killing more of the allied soldiers than Israel's fighting men did.

God's Supernatural Intervention

This vaunted evil alliance was in complete disarray, retreating and being slaughtered on the ground by the Israelites and from the sky by God, in Joshua 10:11–13:

> *And as they fled before Israel, while they were going down the ascent of Beth-horon, the* LORD *threw down large stones from heaven on them as far as Azekah, and they died. There were more who died because of the hailstones than the sons of Israel killed with the sword.* [12] *At that time Joshua spoke to the* LORD *in the day when the* LORD *gave the Amorites over to the sons of Israel, and he said in the sight of Israel, "Sun, stand still at Gibeon, and moon, in the Valley of Aijalon."* [13] *And the sun stood still, and the moon stopped, until the nation took vengeance on their enemies. Is this not written in the Book of Jashar? The sun stopped in the midst of heaven and did not hurry to set for about a whole day.*

When the day faded and Joshua realized he didn't have time before nightfall to finish off the enemy, he asked God for extra time to finish them. As if God joining in the fight hadn't been enough of a miracle, He now provided extended daylight in the valley where the battle unfolded! This was another public display of God's power, bringing creation into subjection to His plan for those who worship Him. It's in the same vein as miracles like the parting of the Red Sea and the

Jordan River, Jesus' transformation of water into wine, and above all, His resurrection. It was yet another story to spread among the rest of the promised land about how the God of Israel was the one true God.

Theology—Gibeonite Armageddon

This whole story is also part of the display of God's grace for the Gibeonites, and His commitment to His people, we saw in the previous chapter.

Put yourself in the place of the Gibeonites. They had only recently joined Joshua and Israel through less-than-ideal means, and already they found themselves facing their Armageddon, an ultimate battle of good versus evil. The evil alliance didn't just oppose them; it despised them for their choice to worship Israel's God. And it was an enemy they couldn't beat on their own. Though they were still like strangers to the Israelites, desperation forced them to ask Joshua to rescue them from this gathering evil. Humanly speaking, Joshua would be risking his entire army against a superior force for people he barely knew. The only hope of Israel and Gibeon alike was for God to show up just in time to rescue His people and defeat this evil alliance.

That's exactly what God did. He told Joshua not to fear, because He would fight for Israel and Gibeon and the evil enemy would be crushed. God fought directly for Israel and Gibeon, causing confusion, sending hailstones, and extending daylight hours. Joshua 10:14 summarizes the significance of this miraculous battle:

Grace for Gibeonites: Who Can Stand Against Us?

There has been no day like it before or since when the LORD heeded the voice of a man, for the LORD fought for Israel.

Why did God participate in this battle in such a unique way? Satan, the real power behind the alliance of five kings, hated how the Gibeonites received grace. Through his demonic influence, he filled these kings with hate and gathered them against the Gibeonites to do his bidding. Satan was the one who really wanted to destroy the Gibeonites after God gathered them. That's why it was an evil alliance.

This is how Satan has been using earthly governments throughout human history, including now in the church age: to create evil alliances against God's people. The enemy has been building evil alliances against the church of Jesus, just as he did at Gibeon. Through Jesus, God has been calling and leading His chosen, adopting us into His covenant, and Satan hates us for it.

God's hand in the battle at Gibeon was like nothing He'd done before and nothing He has done since. But, in a battle yet to take place, this kind of direct divine intervention will occur again. The battle for Gibeon foreshadowed a future conflict described in Revelation 16:13–14 and 16:16:

> *And I saw, coming out of the mouth of the dragon and out of the mouth of the beast and out of the mouth of the false prophet, three unclean spirits like frogs.* [14] *For they are demonic spirits, performing signs, who go abroad to the kings of the whole world, to assemble them for battle on the great day of God the Almighty.*

> ...¹⁶ *And they assembled them at the place that in Hebrew is called Armageddon.*

The lead-up to the ultimate battle in Revelation also features an evil alliance inspired by rage and formed against all of God's redeemed. From a human perspective, this future evil alliance will also seem insurmountable, but thankfully, humans won't have to fight that battle, either. Revelation 19:13–15 tells us who will appear on the battlefield to fight for us: Jesus!

> *He is clothed in a robe dipped in blood.... ¹⁵ From his mouth comes a sharp sword with which to strike down the nations.... He will tread the winepress of the fury of the wrath of God.*

Just as God did at Gibeon, He will allow Satan to gather evil together as a weapon formed against us, and they will fail. Just as God did at Gibeon, our Jesus will lead the battle over Satan's evil alliance. They don't stand a chance against us! Jesus will arrive, leading heaven's armies, and He will be the one to face that alliance and strike it down, like He did at Gibeon. Our Jesus will destroy that evil alliance, and His white robe will be splattered with their blood. The sun did not set until God's judgment was complete at Gibeon, and the same is true with the Day of the Lord, which will be Satan's longest day. No matter how powerful the alliance he forms against us, he will fail in the final confrontation.

Both battles, in Joshua and in Revelation, teach us how to see the world around us, as nations form alliances through history. We know these kinds of battles are not against flesh and blood; they're a battle against spiritual forces.

PERSONAL—JESUS FIGHTS FOR US

Evil alliances are gathering against God's people, but don't be afraid! Jesus will fight for us, so we will be "pressed on every side, but not crushed." I'm sure the Gibeonites would have been able to relate to those words Paul wrote almost 1,300 years later. Do you think they felt Paul's confidence as the evil alliance moved against them? How might they have felt about God after the battle, when He had come with His people and fought to save them? Blessed? Unworthy? Loved?

That day, the Gibeonites personally learned how God never leaves or forsakes those who call upon His name. If they held a worship service the next morning, I'll bet it was lit! I can imagine the conversations: "Even though we came to Him in the wrong way, and as new as we are, God still fights for us and saves us from evil!" "We had nothing to fear all along! God always planned for us to be with His people. Even these evil kings couldn't stop it!" " God didn't save us because we deserve it. He saved us for His glory, purpose, and for His great name." Paul understood that kind of elated confidence born from faith and personal experience, writing in Romans 8:31:

> *What then shall we say to these things? If God is for us, who can be against us?*

Maybe the Gibeonites' immense gratitude and awe in the aftermath of the battle inspired them through generations of service, until their descendants were known as the "dedicated ones" of God's temple. As former wretched, sneaky Gibeonites ourselves, we should relate to how God dealt with them. We were all once Gibeonites who desperately called out to God to rescue us from the evil of this world.

This story is also directly connected to how John describes our future, final battle with evil in Revelation. The grace and love God provided the Gibeonites is the same grace and love Jesus provides for His church. God is building His own holy nation as He calls out His chosen from every earthly tribe and people. That holy nation, God's kingdom, His church, becomes a holy alliance that carries the gospel regardless of the evil alliances formed against us—which are inevitable, as Jesus explained in John 15:19:

> ... because you are not of the world, but I chose you out of the world, therefore the world hates you.

Satan hates how God has rescued us from evil. He also hates how God uses us to rescue others who call upon Him. Evil, motivated by hate, will always try to gather around stories of redemption like bugs drawn to light on a sweltering summer night, hoping to rewrite the endings of those stories into failures. Satan will weaponize every government, religion, philosophy, and economic system into his evil alliance. Have you ever seen a group of nations come together in alliance for the sake of the gospel? Of course not. All earthly alliances, good or bad, are for earthly purposes. Only one kingdom, one nation, is committed to the gospel (and no, it's not America). No earthly alliance is worthy of our hope; our allegiance is to the kingdom of God and the church before anything else.

Just as God empowered Joshua's army to provide grace for the Gibeonites, we are God's army of grace sent to those who by faith call upon the Lord for hope and for rescue from this world's evil alliances. And as God answers their call by sending us to them, He arms us for battle, not with a sword, but with the gospel. Each time we come armed with the gospel, God rescues more Gibeonites from Satan's evil alliance just as He did us. No wonder evil is constantly forming alliances against us! Evil hates the work God is calling us to do; the forces of darkness despise the divine calling God has commissioned us to undertake with the gospel. That's why it can feel like we're the Gibeonites, pressed on all sides by evil as we try to follow our Jesus.

But, we already know Jesus has defeated evil at the cross, and that power will be on full display on the Day of the Lord. As the Gibeonites placed their hope in God's protection, we too hope in the promise Jesus will fight for us on that day. We will all follow the Lamb as He makes final work of that and eradicates evil from this world forever. Until then, as the enemy continues to gather evil alliances to thwart God's plan for our redemption, we will just continue to follow the Lamb wherever He goes.

CHAPTER SEVENTEEN

Land Left to Conquer
(Joshua 10:16–13:7)

Why do people become part of a church? What are the expectations we particularly, as Americans, have when we come to church? Some expect the church to be part of a recipe for a "blessed" life, whatever that might look like to them. We expect the church to help us in recovery, build strong families, unlock the secrets to peace of mind, and much more. These things can be ancillary benefits, but did you know they aren't even in the top five missions for the church?

We must recognize the purpose of the church as so much more than providing earthly blessings. Your moment in time within the church of Jesus is a very small part of God's overall plan of redemption. God did not create His church for your benefit; it was designed with a transcendent purpose far beyond your agenda. It's about our part in this marathon battle against the tide of evil, stretching across the history of redemption. Get ready, because my loving challenge to you is to become part of the real purpose of the church.

HISTORY—BATTLE HARDENED

Joshua's Winning Streak

Joshua 10:15 through chapter 12 records a lengthy list of Joshua's amazing run of military victories over one king after another. After destroying the first evil alliance at Gibeon, Joshua took control of their defenseless cities south of Gibeon, including Makkedah, Gezer, Libnah, Eglon, Lachish, Hebron, and Debir. Other Canaanite kings did not learn from this; they didn't choose to repent and become part of Israel. Instead, in chapter 11, eleven kings and people-groups in the north heard about Gibeon and formed a truly massive alliance. Their army was compared to the sands of the sea, a relentless swarm of enemy forces surrounding Israel on all sides, including Hazor, Shimron, Achshaph, the northern hill country, the Arabah, Naphoth-dor, the Canaanites, the Amorites, the Hittites, the Perizzites, the Jebusites, the Hivites, and the Girgashites (Joshua 11:1–3). But, God fought for Israel again, and they destroyed this alliance, taking all of those hostile cities as well. Each time Satan gathered an alliance of evil against God's people, the Israelites' enemies were all defeated.

These campaigns in the north and south took several decades, as Joshua and Israel defeated city after city. The list of victories they compiled was stunning. Joshua 12 recaps all those defeated by both Moses and Joshua, including Sihon, Og, Jericho, Ai, Jerusalem, Hebron, Jarmuth, Lachish, Eglon, Gezer, Debir, Geder, Hormah, Arad, Libnah, Adullam, Makkedah, Bethel, Tappuah, Hepher, Aphek, Lasharon, Madon, Hazor, Shimron, Meron, Achshaph, Taanach, Megiddo, Kedesh, Jokneam of Carmel, Dor, Gilgal, and Tirzah. Clearly, Israel had effective control of the land, and stories about God spread throughout the regions. However, this didn't mean all the Canaanites were gone. They would always be among God's people, in constant opposition. There were still many lands to the west, toward the Mediterranean Sea, and to the north, but Joshua wouldn't be able to finish the conquest. Moses and Joshua accomplished so much in their lifetimes, yet God's plan was more than two people could accomplish.

Joshua Retires from the Field

In Joshua 13:1–7, God broke it to Joshua that his days of impressive military victory were at an end:

> *Now Joshua was old and advanced in years, and the* LORD *said to him, "You are old and advanced in years, and there remains yet very much land to possess. ... ⁶... I myself will drive them out from before the people of Israel. Only allot the land to Israel for an inheritance, as I have commanded you. ⁷ Now therefore*

> *divide this land for an inheritance to the nine tribes and half the tribe of Manasseh."*

Remember, this was ancient warfare—no tanks, trucks, or Blackhawks. It required decades of fighting to take all those regions. Joshua had been strong and courageous in clearing the land promised to Israel, for which he was revered and beloved. Yet, God described Joshua as "advanced in years." (You know you're old if God calls you old.) Joshua's fighting days were finished; other tribes and leaders would need to pick up his burden from this point forward.

So, Joshua transitioned from military leader to executive organizational leader, preparing Israel for success to come. It wasn't like when the Israelites first entered Canaan with no cities of their own and nothing to lose. In Joshua's new administrative role, he divided the many conquered and unconquered territories among the tribes. This laid the groundwork for growth and stability, a legacy of resilience and hope for future generations of God's people. Joshua trained, organized, and advised the Israelites, preparing them to continue what God had called them to, because His plan was not to unite Israel under one leader anymore. Instead, God wanted Israel to look more like the church today.

THEOLOGY—GOD'S PLAN CONTINUES

Another Evil Alliance

The newer, bigger alliance against Joshua and the Israelites is a clear link to visions John wrote about in Revelation. For instance, the evil nature of this massive second alliance of pagan kings to the north helps us understand Revelation 9:3–11:

> *Then from the smoke came locusts on the earth, and they were given power like the power of scorpions of the earth.* ⁴ *They were told not to harm the grass of the earth or any green plant or any tree, but only those people who do not have the seal of God on their foreheads.* ... ⁷ *In appearance the locusts were like horses prepared for battle: on their heads were what looked like crowns of gold; their faces were like human faces....* ¹¹ *They have as king over them the angel of the bottomless pit.*

The second evil alliance foreshadowed the truths Revelation conveys about facing evil forces in the church age. Evil always comes in terrible waves, because Satan hates God's kingdom and how He continues to call His redeemed. The enemy gathers nations and earthly powers against God's redeemed, and they come at us in droves, like locusts. Some of those hostile forces come from within, so we don't always identify them immediately. The second, swarming alliance in the book of Joshua is an example of how evil operates even today, until our Jesus returns to vanquish evil forever.

Work Yet to Be Finished

The land left for the Israelites to conquer was literal territory, but it also serves as a metaphor for the church's perpetual fight and struggle against evil. For years, Joshua was in the battle for Israel against one evil host after another, defeating every enemy in turn. But, the job wasn't done; there were still parts of the land Joshua was not able to go forth and conquer. The job was too big for one man's lifetime, and the multitudes of darkness would always be a constant threat. It reminds me of what the 144,000 in Revelation represent: the church on earth in battle at any moment in history, relying on Jesus to lead us into unreached places no matter how powerful the forces of evil might be. Paul described this ongoing spiritual conflict in 2 Corinthians 10:4–6:

> *For the weapons of our warfare are not of the flesh but have divine power to destroy strongholds.* ⁵ *We destroy arguments and every lofty opinion raised against the knowledge of God, and take every thought captive to obey Christ,* ⁶ *being ready to punish every disobedience, when your obedience is complete.*

Joshua's role transition and Israel's continuing battle foreshadow our commission to go into all the earth after Jesus ascended. God's promise to Joshua is the same promise Jesus made when He commanded His disciples to go into the land with the Good News. Evil will always attempt to surround God's people, Jesus taught us in the parable of the wheat and the weeds (see Matthew 13: 24–30), but through our Spirit-led proclamation of the gospel, we are driving out evil swarms across the earth.

Since Jesus ascended with a promise to return for the ultimate battle against evil, His church has been through a lot. The forces of evil are constantly swarming around us, using every weapon in their arsenal to fight against what God called us to do. Yet, even when it seemed like evil was insurmountable, the gospel could not be stopped. Jesus said the gates of hell will not prevail, in Matthew 16:18, which implies our enemy is hiding behind his gates. The church is not designed for hunkering down in fear; we are part of a spiritual kingdom on the offensive!

Personal—Our Battle Continues

Until Jesus returns, the church remains in battle, with lands to possess through the proclamation of the gospel. But, Jesus is keeping His promise: no weapon formed will stop His kingdom's advance. The list of evil alliances God and the church have defeated over the last two thousand years is even longer than the list in Joshua. We keep spreading the gospel. Each time the enemy swarms against God's army, He stands up for His people and slaps evil down, and the church goes on. The kingdom advances; evil gathers; it's slapped away. And with this cycle, some of us grow old, advanced in years like Joshua. Our commission likewise includes organizing, training, and structuring to equip the next generation to fight future battles, as Paul taught in 2 Timothy 2:1–3:

> *You then, my child, be strengthened by the grace that is in Christ Jesus, ² and what you have heard from me in the presence of many witnesses entrust to faithful men who will be able to teach others also. ³ Share in suffering as a good soldier of Christ Jesus.*

Despite the extensive list of victories by the church, the good soldiers of Christ Jesus, over two millennia, our war against evil in this fallen world continues. It will persist until our Jesus returns and all those He has chosen before the world began have been saved. In the meantime, no matter how much evil comes against us, it won't stop what God has called us to do as we carry His gospel into the land. God keeps His promise to never leave or forsake us, but to fight for us as we go into unconquered lands. Then, one day a final, massive alliance of evil will arise, and as He has done before, Jesus will defeat it with just His word. The enemy will be destroyed, never to swarm again, and all of us will be with our Jesus, ruling with Him forever.

When he wrote to Timothy, Paul knew his time on this earthly battlefield was almost done. Like Joshua, he wanted to prepare the next generation to take over the fight; he wanted Timothy to be ready for any evil swarm that would form against the church. Paul knew what many people have forgotten: the church isn't designed to be your path to earthly blessings, or "better living through Jesus" as a friend of mine calls it. It's not an evangelical self-help support group, a provider of parenting techniques, or a spiritual hospital to let sick people heal. The primary purpose of discipleship, following Jesus, isn't to help you get your life together and receive God's earthly blessings. The church is God's active army on earth, advancing His kingdom through the proclamation of the gospel to all nations. Discipleship is about preparation for battle as the kingdom advances; it's about taking up your role in the ranks and then passing your responsibilities to those who will keep fighting after God retires you from the field.

For better or worse, each generation does its best to carry the burden of this cosmic battle of redemption. Paul listed the soldierly duties of a Christ-follower in 2 Timothy 4:1–2:

> *I charge you in the presence of God and of Christ Jesus, who is to judge the living and the dead, and by his appearing and his kingdom: ² preach the word; be ready in season and out of season; reprove, rebuke, and exhort, with complete patience and teaching.*

At the same time, it is crucial to equip those who follow to carry on in this way, just as previous generations have done for us. I've had Joshuas in my life who fought many battles, became advanced in years, and turned the fight over to me. God willing, I have many years left of preaching, loving, and serving, but one day, I and many others in the church will be like Joshua, advanced in years. (Some say I already am.) When that moment comes, unless our Jesus returns first, there will be land yet to conquer with the gospel of grace. If you're younger, one day—maybe sooner than you think—you'll need to be ready to take over the battle.

This I can tell you from personal experience: the call to go into the land with the gospel is an exciting privilege. I can also tell you evil has, does, and will continue to swarm around us like locusts as we go into the land. And just as Joshua, one man, couldn't bring the final victory for Israel, we can't either, but Jesus will! Until that day, if you are part of the church, you are called to something deeper than evangelical self-help. The church isn't a "better living with Jesus" seminar. You are part of a church warring against a tide of evil! You are called to be a full participant, part of the church in battle, proclaiming the gospel in this land given to us.

Like Joshua, the older generation needs to equip those behind us with every lesson, tool, experience, and advantage we can. But, the younger generations must show up, learning what they need to learn, so they can be prepared and ready at any moment. Because this very moment, evil swarms everywhere, and there's land left for us to conquer with the power of the gospel.

CHAPTER EIGHTEEN

Wasting an Inheritance
(Joshua 13:8–19:51 & 21:1–42)

Do you think we might be in danger of becoming complacent? We've certainly been blessed, haven't we? As followers of Jesus, we know God has blessed us and given us the gift of faith, the ability to hear when He calls us. We've received the benefits of forgiveness, redemption, and restoration. We've experienced and witnessed transformation. Many of us have seen our church communities grow and our ministries expand. Corporately, we have accomplished a lot, and some of the individuals who have carried much of the burden are, quite understandably, tired. There are many reasons a community of believers falls into the trap of complacency, laziness, and possibly selfishness. Every church comes to a place where its people are tempted to be consumers of our inheritance of grace rather than proclaimers of it. The question is, are there seasons when that's okay?

HISTORY—JOSHUA DIVIDES THE LAND

After years of progress, Israel now had effective power and authority over the land God had given them. In Joshua 13:8 through chapter 19, Joshua followed divine guidance in dividing up both seized and unseized lands among the tribes. All the tribes needed to do was go take it. God commanded a complete takeover because the sins of the Canaanites were fully committed to obscene forms of evil and wickedness; they were beyond hope.

What happened next set in motion generations of slow spiritual decay for Israel. Once they got into their land, they got comfortable and found excuses not to carry the responsibility of obedience, which they now saw as a burden. Instead of living out their purpose, the people of Israel slowly embraced the same evil as the Canaanites. We see their complacency at work in Joshua 13:13:

> *But the people of Israel did not drive out the Geshurites or the Maacathites, but Geshur and Maacath dwell in the midst of Israel to this day.*

And we see it also in Joshua 15:63:

> *But the Jebusites, the inhabitants of Jerusalem, the people of Judah could not drive out, so the Jebusites dwell with the people of Judah at Jerusalem to this day.*

Not only that, but the Israelites also used their inheritance to oppress others for their benefit, as with the people of Gezer in Joshua 16:10:

> *However, they did not drive out the Canaanites who lived in Gezer, so the Canaanites have lived in the midst of Ephraim to this day but have been made to do forced labor.*

This failure was so colossal, Scripture points it out repeatedly: Judges 1:27, Judges 2:1–3, Judges 3:5–6, 1 Kings 11:1–8, and Psalm 106:34–36. Slowly, Israel became addicted to Canaanite idolatry, immorality, sexual exploitation, and human trafficking. From temple prostitutes and human exploitation, both sexually and economically, it all made its way into Israel's culture. Judges 17 gives an example of a man who started his own orgy-based religion and hired a Levite priest to run it! But thankfully, there is a contrasting story of hope in this narrative, which brings us to Joshua 14:6–13:

> *And Caleb the son of Jephunneh the Kenizzite said to him [Joshua], "You know what the LORD said to Moses the man of God ... concerning you and me. ⁷ I was forty years old when Moses the servant of the LORD sent me ... to spy out the land, and I brought him word again as it was in my heart. But my brothers who went up with me made the heart of the people melt; yet I wholly followed the LORD my God. ⁹ And Moses swore on that day, saying, 'Surely the land on which your foot has trodden shall be an inheritance for you and your children forever, because you have wholly followed the*

LORD my God.'¹⁰ And now, behold, the LORD has kept me alive, just as he said, these forty-five years since the time that the LORD spoke this word to Moses, while Israel walked in the wilderness. And now, behold, I am this day eighty-five years old. ¹¹ I am still as strong as I was in the day that Moses sent me; my strength now is as my strength was then, for war and for going and coming. ¹² So now give me this hill country of which the LORD spoke on that day, for you heard how the Anakim were there, with great fortified cities. It may be that the LORD will be with me, and I shall drive them out just as the LORD said." ¹³ Then Joshua blessed him, and he gave Hebron to Caleb the son of Jephunneh for an inheritance.

While the rest of Israel failed to be obedient and follow Joshua's example, Caleb remained faithful, as he always had. When Moses sent his twelve spies out, only Joshua and Caleb believed God would give Israel the land and wanted to go into it. The rest were afraid, because they didn't believe God would keep His promises and they wanted to stay comfortable in the wilderness. Their advice caused a full generation to die in the wilderness, which delayed Israel's inheritance for forty years.

Now, at eighty-five years old, Caleb believed God had kept him just as strong for battle as he was at forty for a specific reason. Hebron was a choice place, but it was also full of evil they'd have to drive out for the land to be redeemed. Caleb didn't want to settle for a comfortable field by the sea of Galilee; he wanted the land God promised him! As laziness crept in among the Israelites, Caleb continued to believe God would keep His promise and use him as His instrument to redeem the hill country of Hebron.

THEOLOGY—TWO TYPES OF HEIRS

Ungrateful Heirs

This part of the Israelites' story was not just about inheriting land. God was using Israel as an instrument of judgment and to proclaim redemption, the same role Jesus intended for us when He commanded us to go into all nations with a gospel that judges and redeems. Yet, after all Israel had seen God do, those tribes decided not to finish what He had commanded them. Right on the cusp of their inheritance, they only needed to go and take it! But, they preferred to coast instead. It seems most of the Israelites either didn't believe in God and His promises or simply stopped caring about their calling. Apparently, most of Israel was only in the fight for their earthly blessings. Once they got the land, they were done. It's just like the prodigal son who, once he got his inheritance, left his father's house to live the life he wanted to live, in Luke 15:12–13:

> *And the younger of them said to his father, "Father, give me the share of property that is coming to me." And he divided his property between them. ¹³ Not many days later, the younger son gathered all he had and took a journey into a far country, and there he squandered his property in reckless living.*

Somehow, the nation of Israel assumed their inheritance was just for them, but that's not what God had in mind. Even after God had shown His power and love and given them this inheritance, their ungratefulness was on full display. It's the same with ungrateful Christians today who profess to follow Jesus but just want the earthly benefits. In both cases, ungratefulness leads to a life bearing no resemblance to the way a follower of God should live. Over the next one thousand years, there would be countless cycles of apostasy, God's restoration, and return to apostasy for Israel. Future generations would make a steady descent into idolatry and every manner of sexual immorality; they would never get to experience the joy that only comes from knowing God and following Him faithfully.

Faithful Caleb

But, there's another side to this story: the grateful obedience from Caleb. He is the example we should follow! Caleb's unwavering faith and vitality, even in his advanced age, stood in contrast to the rest of the lazy, selfish people. What made Caleb different? What made him willing to stay in the fight and risk everything for what God called him to? By faith, Caleb wasn't motivated by selfishness or pleasure, but by the kind of meekness Jesus talked about, in Matthew 5:5:

Blessed are the meek, for they shall inherit the earth.

Part of meekness is humility that puts the welfare of others before its own, recognizing a bigger picture than yourself. Caleb was always able to see beyond his own little world. He knew God's plan benefited him, but he also knew it wasn't about him at all. He understood the inheritance God promised him was not for his benefit; it was about the kingdom of God. Despite his age, Caleb knew God had a job for him: to clear the land God promised him.

One day, God may call you back from the front lines and give you a different role, as with Joshua in his old age. But, both Joshua and Caleb understood, you never retire from God! While the rest of Israel consumed their inheritance for themselves, Caleb saw his inheritance as a path to continuing obedience and service. Caleb understood God had more for him to do and by faith said, "I am ready. I know You're with me, so send me." While the other tribes sought to use their inheritance in a way that fit their agenda, Caleb's desire was for what God wanted. His example is a call to the privilege not only to receive an inheritance but also to participate actively in securing the same for others.

Personal—Faith in Action

Caleb reminds us faith is not for acquiring earthly blessings but for obedience to God's commands. These chapters in Joshua aren't about land but about God equipping His people with what they needed for obedience to His calling. The tension between Israel's failures and Caleb's faithfulness is the same tension we struggle with today in our churches.

This is the complex challenge of following Jesus in a world that wants to tempt us with comfort and complacency.

Our natural tendency is to take what God gives to the church for its mission and instead consume it for ourselves. It's easy to go into the land as Jesus commanded us, find a spot, and settle down, becoming comfortable and complacent. But thankfully, the church has an advantage. The Spirit constantly urges us, pushes us, and prods us toward faithful service, like Paul explained in Ephesians 2:10:

> *For we are his workmanship, created in Christ Jesus for good works, which God prepared beforehand, [so] that we should walk in them.*

Caleb's story is a beautiful example of how God equips and empowers His redeemed for the calling He has for us. What God has done for each of us has prepared us in advance for the unique, special good works He has called us to do. Many of us have faced struggles that tested our faith, but we persevered, confident God had a greater purpose for us. We have adapted to our new calling. We grow spiritually and numerically. Our impact has grown substantially. Just like Israel, we have witnessed firsthand the power of God. It's stunning what He has done for us! We aren't perfect, but we're strong and healthy, so we must remain vigilant against complacency.

One of my fears is becoming so comfortable as God's people, we taste enough of our inheritance and become a prodigal community—distracted and drifting, leaving part of our inheritance unclaimed. We will know when this starts to happen: it always starts when people neglect gathering in community, when we compromise our message, and when we become lazy or, worse, selfish with all the resources God has given us. Can you imagine the impact such drifting would have on future generations in this world we've inherited?

It's easy for any community to reach a stage where it turns its focus inward rather than reaching out to the rest of the world. My worry is that the churches become like the tribes of Israel—settling down, compromising, and neglecting our God-given mission. Will we become content with growth and better finances, or are we, like Caleb, hungry for what God has called us to? The tribes of Israel, when they settled into their lands, started making excuses. We must watch for such signs we might be getting lazy, comfortable, and complacent, the seeds of neglecting our calling. God has not given us all this inheritance just so we could find a place in the land and become comfortable church people! Paul exhorted Jesus-followers in Colossians 3:23–24:

> *Whatever you do, work heartily, as for the Lord and not for men,* [24] *knowing that from the Lord you will receive the inheritance as your reward. You are serving the Lord Christ.*

Are there signs you have started to waste your redemption inheritance on yourself instead of for God's kingdom? Have you entered the land just for earthly blessings? Or, are you still fully committed to what God has called us to do? We have been given a beautiful, rugged hill country that needs to be taken over with our proclamation of the gospel. Just as God made Caleb strong at eighty-five, God has made each of us strong, equipping us in a unique way for a special calling. Like Caleb, we have been assigned good works which God prepared beforehand—and some of us are tripping over them. Remember, our good works, combined with our inheritance, are a critical part of God's plan of redemption both in the church and in our wider communities. Paul encouraged the church to remember the inheritance of hope that should inspire our continued obedience in faith, Ephesians 1:18:

> ... *having the eyes of your hearts enlightened, [so] that you may know what is the hope to which he has called you, what are the riches of his glorious inheritance in the saints* ...

The story of Israel and Caleb should likewise inspire us to be on guard against the encroachment of lazy, selfish complacency. We weren't given this inheritance for our own benefit; it's for our part in the kingdom of God. The calling God has given to each church is unique to any other, woven into the fabric of God's redemptive plan. The church may not be able to do some things other communities can, but do you know what? They can't do some of the things the church can! Just as we need those other communities to do their job, they need us to faithfully do ours. There are people who need the gospel in a way only the church, with our special inheritance, is equipped to proclaim. We must remain active participants, not passive recipients, in what God has called us to do. We must avoid comfortable complacency and keep going into the land, driving out evil through the proclamation of the gospel.

Go into the Land!

CHAPTER NINETEEN

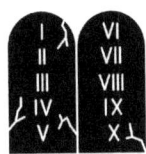

Running to Refuge
(Joshua 20)

Can you imagine being in a position where you were forced to run for your life? Like in the old Western movies where a posse would form and come after you with vigilante justice? I had that same kind of thrill playing childhood games like Capture the Flag. But, what if it were real, and you were running for your life with no refuge, no safe zone? How exhausting! This is the spiritual condition of everyone ever born, even if they don't realize it. Spiritually, we are all running for our lives. Finding refuge where we can escape the real threat is our only hope. Joshua 20 centers on our desperate need for refuge and where to go to find it.

HISTORY—CITIES OF REFUGE

God instructed the Israelites to establish "cities of refuge," explained in Joshua 20:1–9:

Then the LORD said to Joshua, [2] "Say to the people of Israel, 'Appoint the cities of refuge, of which I spoke to you through Moses, [3] [so] that the manslayer who strikes any person without intent or unknowingly may flee there. They shall be for you a refuge from the avenger of blood. [4] He shall flee to one of these cities and shall stand at the entrance of the gate of the city and explain his case to the elders of that city. Then they shall take him into the city and give him a place, and he shall remain with them. [5] And if the avenger of blood pursues him, they shall not give up the manslayer into his hand, because he struck his neighbor unknowingly, and did not hate him in the past. [6] And he shall remain in that city until he has stood before the congregation for judgment, until the death of him who is high priest at the time. Then the manslayer may return to his own town and his own home, to the town from which he fled.'"

[7] So they set apart Kedesh in Galilee in the hill country of Naphtali, and Shechem in the hill country of Ephraim, and Kiriath-arba (that is, Hebron) in the hill country of Judah. [8] And beyond the Jordan east of Jericho, they appointed Bezer in the wilderness on the tableland, from the tribe of Reuben, and Ramoth in Gilead, from the tribe of Gad, and Golan in Bashan, from the tribe of Manasseh. [9] These were the cities

designated for all the people of Israel and for the stranger sojourning among them, [so] that anyone who killed a person without intent could flee there, so that he might not die by the hand of the avenger of blood, till he stood before the congregation.

Cities of refuge were a divine provision from God, an expression of how His justice and mercy would be different. God made this provision because He knew humans have a thirst for vengeance. This system put vengeance on hold until the situation could be evaluated, and justice served proportionately. The book of Numbers contains God's command given years beforehand for what these cities would be, including this explanation in Numbers 35:10–15:

> *Speak to the people of Israel and say to them, When you cross the Jordan into the land of Canaan, [11] then you shall select cities to be cities of refuge for you, [so] that the manslayer who kills any person without intent may flee there. [12] The cities shall be for you a refuge from the avenger, [so] that the manslayer may not die until he stands before the congregation for judgment. [13] And the cities that you give shall be your six cities of refuge. [14] You shall give three cities beyond the Jordan, and three cities in the land of Canaan, to be cities of refuge. [15] These six cities shall be for refuge for the people of Israel, and for the stranger and for the sojourner among them, [so] that anyone who kills any person without intent may flee there."*

These six cities of refuge were among forty-eight cities throughout Canaan given to the Levitical priests instead of land. They were strategically located so no matter where you were, a city of refuge was never more than a day's journey away. They provided a place of safety always within reach for anyone who might need it—even sojourners and pagans.

Here's how these places of refuge worked: If someone was accidentally killed, their family had the right to hold the killer responsible. Often, an "avenger of blood" was appointed, usually a family member with the responsibility to bring the killer to justice. This avenger would gather a posse to pursue and hunt the accused down and take revenge on behalf of the family. The accused had two choices: to run or to form their own posse and begin a brutal blood feud, an Israelite version of the Hatfields and McCoys. Blood feuds extended to all family members, lasting for generations. Cities of refuge could prevent the bloody cycle, providing a way for the accused to avoid the fight and seek protection and restoration.

God's plan entailed the elders of the city hearing the case. If they ruled the death was a murder, the killer was turned over to the "avenger of blood" for justice. But, if the elders ruled the death was accidental, the accused was given safe refuge if he remained in the city. If the accused left the city, the "avenger of blood" would then be lawfully allowed to take revenge. However, once the sitting high priest died, the slate for all refuge cases in every city was wiped clean. Over this period, emotions had cooled, the thirst for revenge had waned, and healing might have occurred. The accused, by law, could then leave the city and return home without fear of retribution from the avenger of blood, who would be liable for murder if he enacted revenge after that.

THEOLOGY—A GOD OF REFUGE

The theme of God providing refuge for His people, in His overwhelming mercy and grace, occurs constantly throughout Scripture. The Israelites' cities of refuge provide many glimpses of Jesus, the ultimate safe harbor for sinners and His church.

The Need for Refuge

Why did Israel need six cities of refuge for accidental killings in the first place? How many accidental deaths must be occurring to justify six strategically placed cities of refuge never more than a day away? The need for so many places of refuge for unintentional killing speaks to the depravity of the human heart, described in Psalm 14:2-3:

> *The LORD looks down from heaven on the children of man, to see if there are any who understand, who seek after God. ³ They have all turned aside; together they have become corrupt; there is none who does good, not even one.*

Despite all He had done for His people, God knew depravity would have an impact on them and on justice among them. Every sin, even accidental unintentional ones, are by-products of the power of sin in us to twist and malign our lives. They all carry some sort of earthly consequence for all of us, but also eternal consequences for the unredeemed. Part of human depravity is injustice in society.

The list of ways God provided the Israelites a path to mercy, justice, and restoration is long, and cities of refuge were one of many. These cities of refuge prevented injustice or vigilante justice. Not everyone needed a city of refuge, but when you did, you were glad it was close by—and you ran there fast! The need for these cities reveals how all of us, whether we know it or not, desperately need grace, mercy, and refuge.

Blood Avenger

The role of the blood avenger reminds us that the consequences of our sin are real and all around us. Paul contrasted the gravity of sin with the grace of God, in Romans 6:23:

> *For the price of sin is death, but the free gift of God is eternal life in Christ Jesus our Lord.*

The blood avenger, like the law, demanded justice and retribution for sin: an eye for an eye, a life for a life. Without protection or refuge from the law's thirst for justice, one day the consequences of sin will catch up to us all.

The High Priest's Death

The death of the high priest wiping the slate clean carries critical theological importance. The goal of the cities of refuge wasn't merely temporary safety but to provide a path to complete restoration. If you were innocent, you initially wanted to escape the blood avenger, but then you wanted to be cleared and restored. This part of the law concerning the cities of refuge and the high priest made ultimate restoration possible. Once the high priest died, the accused was free to return home with protection from the law, and peace was restored.

When it comes to sin, God's purpose is the same. He provides a path for our restoration to make things right. This restoration is also accomplished through the death of a high priest—the ultimate High Priest, our Jesus, as explained in Hebrews 2:17:

> *Therefore he had to be made like his brothers in every respect, so that He might become a merciful and faithful high priest in the service of God, to make propitiation [die as payment] for the sins of the people.*

Jesus, our great high priest, died on the cross, wiping away every sin of His people—past, present, and future. Christ's death and resurrection, declared through the gospel, offers restoration and healing from all the sin you carry!

Run by Priests

These cities of refuge, unlike other cities, were given to the priests to live in and govern. They were run by those whom God designated to be the intercessors between Him and His people. Who has been given responsibility to oversee our place of refuge, the church? First Peter 2:9 points to the answer: us, a nation of royal priests:

> *But you are a chosen race, a royal priesthood, a holy nation, a people for his own possession, [so] that you may*

proclaim the excellencies of him who called you out of darkness into his marvelous light.

Jesus has made His church a city of refuge in the way we proclaim His good news to all, making His truth accessible to all who need it. We invite the world around us, "Find refuge, restoration, and healing here, in this safe place."

Never Far from Refuge

The cities of refuge were close, never more than a day's journey away. Likewise, the gospel is accessible to all who believe, Paul wrote in Romans 10:13:

> . . . *for "everyone who calls on the name of the Lord will be saved."*

The refuge of the gospel is always just a prayer away, closer than a day's journey. Those in need of Jesus can bring themselves to His place of refuge anytime, anywhere!

PERSONAL—JESUS IS OUR REFUGE

There is one glaring difference between the cities of refuge and the refuge Christ offers us through the gospel. These cities were a provision for those who were not guilty of murder to have a chance at justice. But our depravity runs so deep, our lives are filled with unintentional sin, not to mention intentional sin. Because of this sin, we desperately need a place of refuge. Thankfully, the refuge Jesus offers is for the guilty, and it's available at any time, in any place. Jesus is a refuge even after the fact, when we who follow Him fail! His promises offer encouragement and hope for those who, like Hebrews 6:18 says, run in repentance to His refuge of forgiveness:

> ... *we who have fled for refuge might have strong encouragement to hold fast to the hope set before us.*

And one day, when our Jesus returns to eradicate evil, He will provide our ultimate, eternal refuge from evil. In the meantime, do people see the church as a place of refuge, a voice calling them to run for a reprieve from the judgment we all deserve? If Jesus has become your refuge, the evidence will be your insatiable desire to provide refuge for others running for their lives. You won't just sit comfortably within the walls of grace and mercy; you'll be inspired to invite others into this refuge. That's what makes the church a beautiful city: it's a collection of guilty sinners who found refuge from what we deserve and are now driven by a desire to call out to others, inviting them to find the refuge that is never far away!

We are the sanctuary of refuge for souls seeking to be rescued from the penalty of sin. God has called this vast global network of royal priests and positioned us strategically throughout church history. He has called us out of darkness, into light, and made us accessible to every nation and culture. The world around us may not know it, but the church is their only hope. We provide an open door for everyone, regardless of their past, present, or circumstances. We who have run for refuge in Jesus should be calling out to those around us:

"Run! Run to Jesus before it's too late! Come join us in this city of refuge we call Jesus and His church!"

Many of you reading this have found, within the church, refuge and restoration from the eternal consequences of your sins. We understand the truth of Psalm 62:7–8:

> *On God rests my salvation and my glory; my mighty rock, my refuge is God. ⁸ Trust in Him at all times, O people; pour out your heart before Him; God is a refuge for us.*

Or, maybe you've never realized how much you need refuge, though you always knew something wasn't right. You've felt an anxious need to run from the burden of sin you carry within you. Maybe you've been running for a long time, desperately searching for refuge from the consequences and restoration from the guilt of your sin. If so, there's a place of refuge available to you right now. Let Jesus call you out of darkness and into light as you pray to Him for refuge, taking shelter in Him and His church. Run to Him, allowing Him to wipe your slate clean through the cross! In the city of refuge, you'll finally be at home, at rest among His people as we learn, grow, and wait for Jesus to return.

CHAPTER TWENTY

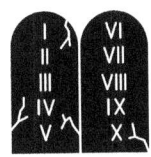

Keeping Promises
(Joshua 21:43–22:9)

Do you believe the modern church is super-faithful and obedient to everything Jesus has commanded us? If you had to rate the faithfulness of the church of Jesus on a scale of 1 to 10 throughout its history, what would it be? Think of all the blunders, embarrassing mistakes, and theological errors. The list of how the church has failed is long.

Next question: on a scale of 1 to 10, how faithful has the church been in spreading the gospel throughout the world? How many millions of people in every nation have been saved through the church preaching God's word? It's pretty clear this movement called the church of Jesus is global, growing, and in many places thriving.

If the church has been so flawed throughout its history, how do we reconcile its faithfulness to the Great Commission? Considering all our challenges, distractions, and weaknesses, how does the church keep advancing faithfully? The church, especially here in America, seems so dysfunctional, yet is still very effective. Let's consider the possibility that the church's faithfulness isn't as reliant upon human effectiveness as we might assume. Perhaps there's a divine force, a faithful promise-keeper, ensuring we're faithful to the mission despite our flaws.

Joshua 21:43–45 reveals the foundational truth that God's people, the Israelites in Canaan and the followers of Jesus in the church today, will remain faithful despite our weakness because our inheritance rests ultimately on God's promises:

> *Thus the LORD gave to Israel all the land that he swore to give to their fathers. And they took possession of it, and they settled there.* ⁴⁴ *And the LORD gave them rest on every side just as he had sworn to their fathers. Not one of all their enemies had withstood them, for the LORD had given all their enemies into their hands.* ⁴⁵ *Not one word of all the good promises that the LORD had made to the house of Israel had failed; all came to pass.*

History—Promises Made and Kept

Undeserved Favor

Since crossing the Jordan under Joshua's leadership, Israel had faced numerous battles and learned many lessons. They'd had many successes, a lengthy list beginning with Jericho, Ai, and Gibeon. Yet, they'd also had many challenges and failures due to their failure to seek God's guidance, incidents like Achan's sin and the deception by the Gibeonites. Israel failed to drive out their enemies completely in Joshua chapters 13 to 20, even though God promised to do it for them. All they had to do was go into all the land, and God would clear it just as He had the rest of Canaan. The Israelites' complacency needlessly prolonged their campaign, wasting years, lives, and resources. And these are only the failures we know about!

Despite their laziness, unfaithfulness, disobedience, dishonesty, and arrogance, God kept His promises at every turn. He gave Israel all the land He promised and defeated every enemy coming against them, no matter how terrifying.

"Ride or Die" Tribes

The old biker phrase "ride or die" has become an affectionate label for someone who proves willing to stick with you no matter what. Whether winning or losing, thriving or struggling, laughing or crying, everyone needs people who are "ride or die." That's what the two and a half tribes addressed in Joshua 22:1–9 were for the rest of the tribes of Israel:

At that time Joshua summoned the Reubenites and the Gadites and the half-tribe of Manasseh, ² *and said to them, "You have kept all that Moses the servant of the* LORD *commanded you and have obeyed my voice in all that I have commanded you.* ³ *You have not forsaken your brothers these many days down to this day, but have careful to keep the charge of the* LORD *your God.* ⁴ *And now the* LORD *your God has given rest to your brothers, as he promised them. Therefore turn and go to your tents in the land where your possession lies, which Moses the servant of the* LORD *gave you on the other side of the Jordan.* ⁵ *Only be very careful to observe the commandment and the law that Moses the servant of the* LORD *commanded you, to love the* LORD *your God, and to walk in all his ways, and to keep his commandments and to cling to him and to serve him with all your heart and with all your soul."* ⁶ *So Joshua blessed them and sent them away, and they went to their tents.*

⁷ *Now to the one half of the tribe of Manasseh Moses had given a possession in Bashan, but to the other half Joshua had given a possession beside their brothers in the land west of the Jordan. And when Joshua sent them away to their homes and blessed them,* ⁸ *he said to them, "Go back to your tents with much wealth and with very much livestock, with silver, gold, bronze, and iron, and with much clothing. Divide the spoil of your enemies with your brothers."* ⁹ *So the people of Reuben and the people of Gad and the half-tribe of Manasseh returned home, parting from the people of Israel at Shiloh, which is in the land of Canaan, to go to the*

land of Gilead, their own land of which they had possessed themselves by command of the LORD through Moses.

Before Moses died, the tribes of Reuben and Gad and the half-tribe of Manasseh asked Moses for the pasture lands east of the Jordan. They were shepherding tribes, and those plains were ideal for the life they wanted for themselves and their families. Moses granted their request on condition that they would fight with the rest of Israel until all tribes received their inheritance. Later, when Moses was dead and Joshua was about to take over leading Israel into the promised land, he called on them, in Joshua 1:13–15.

The faithfulness of these two and a half tribes, which we learned about in Chapter Two, is one of the most inspirational human aspects of the book of Joshua. This was no small commitment—leaving their families and homes to fight alongside their brothers in Canaan. Their promise cost many of them a significant portion of their adult lives. Some probably died in battle, got sick, or grew old. Now, after years of faithful service to their brothers, the time had come for Joshua to release and reward them.

THEOLOGY—PROMISE KEEPERS

Promise keepers feature heavily in this story, including those two and a half tribes who crossed the Jordan to fight alongside their brothers for many years and, above all, God Himself.

Faithful Men and Women

The fighting men of Reuben, Gad, and Manasseh were faithful and obedient and kept their promises. Their wives and families back home also remained faithful to God while waiting for their men to return. But, how much credit should they get for these good things they did? Clearly, there was a greater power at work here. This is a beautiful Old Testament example of the New Testament truth Paul articulated in Ephesians 2:10, when he described us walking in "good works, which God prepared beforehand."

Before those Israelites could ever even think about keeping their promise, God had to keep His promises. Their faithfulness was, in fact, divinely driven and possible only because God kept His covenant promises first.

God's Promises

Deuteronomy 7:7–9 makes clear that God's covenant relationship with the nation of Israel was founded on His promise-keeping, not theirs:

> It was not because you were more in number than any other people that the LORD set his love on you and chose you, for you were the fewest of all peoples, *8* but it is because the LORD loves you and is keeping the oath that he swore to your fathers, that the LORD has brought you out with a mighty hand and redeemed you from the house of slavery, from the hand of Pharaoh king of Egypt. *9* Know therefore that the LORD your God is God, the faithful God who keeps covenant and

steadfast love with those who love him and keep his commandments, to a thousand generations...

Prior to those promises of a steadfast, loving God, Israel had not done anything to earn or merit His favor—quite the opposite! When God made these promises to Abraham, He wasn't backing a winner by any stretch. They were the most unlikely nation to be able to fulfill all that God had called them to do, yet they did. Even though Israel would often fail miserably to keep their end of the deal, and did the exact opposite of what they were supposed to do, God never failed to keep His promises. The history of the Israelites, including the two and a half tribes, teaches us the foundation of God's relationship with His people relies on His faithfulness, not ours. This story is part of a massive theological narrative throughout all of Scripture that we call covenant theology. His promise-keeping enables the faithfulness and righteousness of His people, because He as a covenant keeper both provides the opportunity for our good works and keeps us faithful.

PERSONAL—ARE WE "RIDE OR DIE"?

When God's people are obedient, it's because God keeps His promises first. Humanly speaking, the Israelites as a whole, and those two and a half tribes in particular, were given an impossible command to enter and conquer Canaan. On their own, they never even would have crossed the Jordan River! They really didn't want to go in the first place. How long would those tribes have remained faithful if God had not parted the Jordan River, defeating Jericho and Ai? Do you think they would have kept their promises if God had not confused that huge alliance of the enemy at Gibeon? Do you think they would have kept their promises if God had not sent hailstones and made the day longer?

On a personal level, are you ever afraid you would not be "ride or die" in what God has called you to do? Do you really think we have any chance of being faithful and obedient on our own, by our own free will? Paul reassured the church, in 1 Thessalonians 5:24, keeping our part of the covenant with God doesn't depend on us:

He who calls you is faithful; he will surely do it.

Our obedience and faithfulness are powered by the same thing enabling Reuben, Gad, and Manasseh's obedience. Just as God kept His promises for them, our Jesus keeps His promise to be with us always, until our calling is completed. The faithfulness of our covenant keeper inspires our gratitude, confidence, and commitment to our mission, as expressed in Hebrews 10:23:

Let us hold fast the confession of our hope without wavering, for he who promised is faithful.

Like the tribes who stood by their brothers, we are called to be "ride or die" for Jesus in this life—and for each other as well, because the church has been given a job far more challenging than conquering Canaan. Jesus has commanded us to go into the world, faithfully proclaiming the gospel until the day He returns. Since Jesus gave us that command, church history is much like Israel's story, replete with examples of human frailty. From bad theology and worldly distractions to moral failures and financial indiscretions, how have we experienced any success?

Despite our failures and weaknesses, the church has been remarkably faithful to our calling. It's only possible because the promises Jesus keeps for us in the new covenant are far superior to His old covenant with Israel. Our connection with God and our obedience to our calling is always a result of Jesus, our covenant keeper, and the foundation of His love, as 1 John 4:19 explains:

We love because he first loved us.

When we are obedient and faithful, we don't take credit for it; we see it as evidence Jesus is keeping His promises! Our faithfulness, reliability, and endurance are a direct result of our Jesus keeping His new covenant promises to us. Because of that, we who follow Him will prove, ultimately, to be ride or die for Jesus and His church. Those who don't prove to be ride or die aren't part of the covenant with Jesus, according to 1 John 2:19:

They went out from us, but they were not of us; for if they had been of us, they would have continued with us.

That's what James meant when, in James 2, he described faith without evidence of transformation and concluded such faith wasn't real. People outside the covenant will be unreliable, unstable, and unfaithful when it comes to God's kingdom. They'll show up occasionally, when it's convenient or beneficial—when the church has something they want or need. But, they won't stick around once the fight gets tough; the allure and temptations of the world will win out. So, you are either "ride or die" for Jesus and His church, or you're unreliable, one or the other. This is why Hebrews 10:23 encourages us to ground our hope and confidence in Jesus.

We have been given a tough job to do as the church, and we will never be faithful without Jesus. There's no way any church would be meeting today if Jesus weren't keeping His promises! There's no way any of us would have the gift of faith to become followers of Jesus if He weren't a faithful promise-keeper. Our faithfulness will always be a result of Him, the great covenant keeper, unwavering in His promise to never leave us. Our obedience is always a response of gratitude to our God who loved us first, when we weren't very lovable. Isn't it a comfort to know that those who follow Jesus, despite our flaws, will stay true to Him? The church stands firm because He is our covenant keeper, who abides by His promises without fail.

CHAPTER TWENTY-ONE

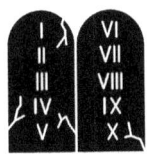

Protecting Unity
(Joshua 22:10–34)

Have you ever seen or been part of a church conflict? Obviously, if a church has too much conflict, that's a sign it isn't healthy, but a church with no conflict isn't a healthy church, either. Often, Christians lack the courage to deal with conflict. In fact, most choose to deal with it in anger or just walk away. We prefer silent or slanderous judgment, cutting people off, avoiding them, looking right past them, or just leaving the church. Others "courageously" confront in anger or self-righteousness. They don't want reconciliation; they want retribution.

As a pastor, I've had a front-row seat to conflict. I've seen it destroy lifelong friendships and families, and even split churches. My wife and I have personally experienced the consequences of conflict handled incorrectly. It's costly and painful every time. When conflict is handled properly, on the other hand, it's an incredible opportunity for love and unity and brings a smile to God's face. How a church handles conflicts provides a window into the spiritual maturity of its leadership and members.

It's no surprise, therefore, that dealing with conflict and protecting unity is one of God's highest priorities. We've already seen as much several times in the book of Joshua, like in the way He dealt with Achan and in His instructions about the six cities of refuge. But, the Israelites were far from finished experiencing division and dissent, and the same would be true of Jesus' followers in the New Testament, too.

HISTORY—CONFLICT IN ISRAEL

Troubling Altar

After the war, the two and a half tribes headed home to the other side of the Jordan. On their way, they stopped before crossing the Jordan River and constructed a massive altar no one could miss. The other ten tribes saw this as a deviation from the worship of the Lord: "Hey, are these guys ditching God?" In response, the ten tribes mustered forces at Shiloh, contemplating war with the eastern tribes who had just fought by their side!

Hoping for a peaceful resolution, the ten tribes sent Phinehas, the son of the high priest, and a leader from each tribe. Phinehas approached the eastern tribes with their concerns, but did so with an attitude of brotherly love. The representatives of the ten tribes recounted how Israel suffered because of Achan's sin, losing the battle of Ai and the men who died there. They recalled a story about sin at Peor in Numbers 25, where thousands of men in Israel were seduced by Moabite and Midianite women, becoming ensnared in rampant sexual immorality and orgy-worship in the temple of Baal. This immorality caused a devastating plague that killed 24,000 Israelites before those guilty were executed. Both tragedies had happened in the past five to ten years; the pain over the consequences was still there.

These stories reminded the two and a half tribes how sin could impact an entire nation, yet Phinehas and the others weren't judgmental. They were concerned unclean sacrifices had made the land east of the Jordan unclean and unfit for the people of God. They were so committed to unity, they offered the eastern tribes new lands if they returned to the west side of the Jordan. They weren't self-righteous or angry, but were genuinely concerned for the unity of God's people!

The eastern tribes explained how they'd rather die by the hand of God than forsake Him or betray their brothers. They made clear that just as they were "ride or die" with their brothers when fighting for Canaan, they were "ride or die" with God. They were afraid future generations would forget how the two and a half tribes had been loyal to their parents. Future generations might think because they lived east of the Jordan that they were enemies, not part of Israel. Their altar wasn't for sacrifices or as a rival to the main altar at Shiloh. Rather, it was a public monument of commitment to God.

Unity Restored

Once the tribes of Reuben, Gad, and Manasseh explained what the altar was for, you can imagine the relief and joy of all the people! Joshua 22:30–34 recounts what happened next:

> *When Phinehas the son of Eleazar the priest and the chiefs of the congregation, the heads of the families of Israel who were with him, heard the words that the people of Reuben and the people of Gad and the people of Manasseh spoke, it was good in their eyes.* ³¹ *And Phinehas the son of Eleazar the priest said to the people of Reuben and the people of Gad and the people of Manasseh, "Today we know that the* LORD *is in our midst, because you have not committed this breach of faith against the* LORD. *Now you have delivered the people of Israel from the hand of the* LORD.*"*
>
> ³² *Then Phinehas the son of Eleazar, and the chiefs, returned from the people ... in the land of Gilead to Canaan, to the people of Israel, and brought back word to them.* ³³ *And the report was good in the eyes of the people of Israel. And the people of Israel blessed God and spoke no more of making war ... to destroy the land where the people of Reuben and the people of Gad were settled.* ³⁴ *The people of Reuben and the people of Gad called the altar Witness, "For," they said, "it is a witness between us that the* LORD *is God."*

The altar became a monument of the eastern tribes' desire to stay connected to God and unified with the rest of Israel.

This conflict resolution also became a testimony to the nations of God's faithfulness and the unity among His people.

THEOLOGY— UNITY IS CONSTANTLY UNDER ATTACK

What would have happened if this conflict spiraled out of control and into a bloody civil war? Everything these tribes had accomplished together would have been wasted, and their futures together destroyed. Doesn't that sound like something forces of evil would be thrilled to see happen? Be assured, the forces of darkness have always despised unified obedience among followers of Jesus. Paul warned us that our fight is not actually with each other but against spiritual forces (see Ephesians 6:12). Just as Satan hates our unity, God upholds it; it's one of His highest priorities. He provides wisdom and patience to avoid disaster, and He is always at work to maintain the unity of His people, despite our propensity to fight with each other.

Conflict Between Peter and Paul

One of the big conflicts in the early years of the church had to do with misguided Jews in the congregation treating Gentile followers of Jesus like second-class believers. They considered uncircumcised Gentile believers "unclean." They wouldn't sit or eat with them at church gatherings. This situation in the Antioch church led Paul into confrontation with

Peter, one of Jesus' original disciples, as he described in Galatians 2:11–14:

> But when Cephas [Peter] came to Antioch, I opposed him to his face, because he stood condemned. ¹² For before certain men came from James, he was eating with the Gentiles; but when they came he drew back and separated himself, fearing the circumcision party. ¹³ And the rest of the Jews acted hypocritically along with him, so that even Barnabas was led astray by their hypocrisy. ¹⁴ But when I saw that their conduct was not in step with the truth of the gospel, I said to Cephas before them all, "If you, though a Jew, live like a Gentile and not like a Jew, how can you force the Gentiles to live like Jews?"

Even though Peter knew salvation wasn't through works or the law, he'd been afraid to oppose the circumcision party. When he failed to stand up for the Gentiles, it must have been very discouraging for them. Frankly, it was a real mess. Satan certainly tried to exploit this conflict, using it to attack church unity as he loves to do. But, God gave Paul wisdom and courage to address the conflict in a way that brought beautiful reconciliation.

Paul didn't gossip, condemn, or complain to others about Peter in private. He addressed Peter directly in Antioch. For his part, did Peter get angry and cut Paul off? No—he repented! The evidence is in his letters to the churches in Asia Minor Paul planted. His letters 1 Peter and 2 Peter are full of bold statements about how Gentile believers were full citizens in the kingdom of God. All those Peter failed to confront initially would have either read or heard of Peter's declarations about the Gentiles: they were not second-class citizens; they were as much a part of the royal priesthood as any Jewish follower of Jesus.

Apostolic Unity

Peter went further in his epistles and affirmed the apostolic authority of everything Paul taught, in 2 Peter 3:15–16:

> ...*just as our beloved brother Paul also wrote to you according to the wisdom given him,* [16] *as he does in all his letters when he speaks in them of these matters. There are some things in them that are hard to understand, which the ignorant and unstable twist to their own destruction, as they do the other Scriptures.*

The reconciliation between Paul and Peter had preserved unity and led to an explosion of the gospel among Gentiles. Years later, when Paul knew his time on earth was coming to an end, he wrote about his pending death in his letters. He expressed deep affection for the Gentile churches he'd started as well as concern for their health after he was gone. Paul wrote many other letters we don't know about, and it's no stretch to think he urged surviving apostles to care for the precious Gentile believers, guiding and teaching them. After Paul died, Peter and John stepped up big-time, from what we read in Peter's two epistles and John's three epistles. These great letters are a direct product of God protecting the unity of His people in ways we continue to benefit from today.

Personal—Protecting Our Unity

Jesus made the unity of His followers one of our highest priorities. Sadly, we make it one of our most neglected. But, God knew we, His people, would struggle with conflict as we follow His command to go into the land. We are human! Throughout church history, it seems one of the greatest obstacles God's people have faced has been conflict with each other. Sometimes, it's the result of our own individual sin or disobedience. Other times, it's because of a misunderstanding. But, we know from Jesus how much He hates disunity among His people, whether it's from misunderstanding or sin. He said so directly, in Matthew 5:22–24:

> *But I say to you that everyone who is angry with his brother will be liable to judgment; whoever insults his brother will be liable to the council; and whoever says, "You fool!" will be liable to the hell of fire.* [23] *So if you are offering your gift at the altar and there remember your brother has something against you,* [24] *leave your gift there before the altar and go. First be reconciled to your brother, and then come and offer your gift.*

Were you aware just how seriously Jesus takes this issue of unity? Do you see the warnings He lays out? Let me be clear: you don't have the right *not* to deal with it. I'm not saying that; it's our Jesus saying it. The consequences of disunity and conflict are devastating corporately, but also for each of us personally. Indeed, the records of both confrontations we've examined in this chapter—between the ten tribes and the two and a half tribes and between Paul and Peter—reveal to us how seriously God takes the issue of unity among His people.

So, if reconciliation and protecting unity are this important, what are you supposed to do? Phinehas's resolution of the altar incident, and Paul's confrontation with Peter over the Gentile controversy, provide critical instruction in principles of conflict resolution for God's people to follow. And Jesus Himself told us clearly what to do, in Matthew 18:15–17:

> *If your brother sins against you, go and tell him his fault, between you and him alone. If he listens, you have gained your brother. [16] But if he does not listen, take one or two others along with you, [so] that every charge may be established by the evidence of two or three witnesses. [17] If he refuses to listen to them, tell it to the church. And if he refuses to listen even to the church, let him be to you as a Gentile and a tax collector [an unbeliever].*

Sadly, I've seen churches abuse this process Jesus detailed, using it not for reconciliation and unity but for retribution or public ridicule. That's so destructive and not what our Jesus intended. His goal is always love and unity, not revenge and anger. If you have an issue with a brother or sister, don't sit in bitterness or gossip or slander them; confront them privately. If you can reconcile, unity is restored. If not, take one or two mediators. If you reconcile now, unity is restored. If you still can't find reconciliation, bring it to the church leaders. If you can reconcile, unity is preserved. And after all that, if there's no reconciliation, we are to consider the other person an outsider.

What does that mean? It doesn't mean you get to cut them off, judge them, or stay angry and bitter for years. No, you are to love them. You are to treat them as someone who needs to experience the gospel! Preach the gospel to them in love. But, what if someone does the same thing over and over? Well, that answer comes just a couple of verses later, in Matthew 18:21–22:

> *Then Peter came up and said to him, "Lord, how often will my brother sin against me, and I forgive him? As many as seven times?" ²² Jesus said to him, "I do not say to you seven times but seventy-seven times."*

You are to walk through the same process seventy times seven times. So at 491, maybe you're allowed to be bitter and angry forever. (If you think I'm serious there, you might be missing the point.) James encouraged Jesus' followers to persist in correcting one another in truth and love, as Paul did for Peter, in James 5:19–20:

> *My brothers, if anyone among you wanders from the truth and someone brings him back, ²⁰ let him know that whoever brings back a sinner from his wandering will save his soul from death and will cover a multitude of sins.*

The problem is, most of us won't even go through this process once, let alone 490 times. I struggle with this myself, because our natural human tendency is to just be angry and bitter. It seems much easier.

In some cases, though, reconciliation may not be possible. What then? You'd better pray and live in a silent state of forgiveness; otherwise, the cancers of bitterness and resentment take over, evil gains a foothold, and our commission is compromised.

As followers of Jesus, we need to protect our unity and love for one another zealously. This is practical! We must have the courage necessary to address these issues in love (not anger) and look for resolution. Our job of going into the land with the gospel is hard, so we cannot make it harder by destroying our unity and fighting with one another. To be successful as we go into the land with the gospel, we must have vulnerable, courageous, humble conversations. This is a test of your faith. Don't rationalize continued inaction!

Is there unresolved conflict right now in your church family? Maybe it's been that way for years, but you don't have the option to do nothing any longer, because Jesus said clearly what you must do. Obedience requires action.

CHAPTER TWENTY-TWO

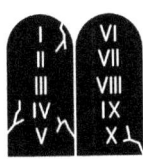

Teaching the Next Generation
(Joshua 23)

Do you remember earlier, after Jericho and Ai, when outsiders were drawn to Mt. Ebal to join Israel in worshiping God? I believe every church must become like Mt. Ebal, where the hurting and the seeking are drawn to experience redemption. Yet, as more sojourners gather, natural and sometimes healthy subgroups form. There are children and younger families, young adults, and older saints who've known Jesus for a long time. There are women's groups, men's groups, single moms, married parents, and those in recovery ministries.

The problem is when these subgroups form barriers and have little to no interaction with each other. They may even resent each other. When these barriers form, they become big obstacles to the success of our mission. A growing church must become more intentional about the relationships forming within its community.

In the previous chapter, we learned the importance of protecting and nurturing unity to our success. We learned how important reconciliation and conflict resolution are as crucial parts of protecting and nurturing our unity. This chapter is about another critical ingredient for building powerful, healing, enduring unity for the Great Commission we received from Jesus in Matthew 28:19–20: we must ensure we take down any barriers so they don't get in the way of our calling. One way we must do this is by older generations teaching the younger how to go into the land with the gospel. That's not just a matter of parents instructing their children. It's also about teaching those who can continue our work when we are done.

HISTORY—WISDOM AND WARNINGS

A Farewell Address

Joshua had led Israel for decades and had done everything God had instructed, to the best of his ability. He'd proven to be an effective, seasoned military commander who led Israel through many battles against powerful enemies. But, Joshua knew the battlefield was only one part of the journey, for him and for the Israelites, whose greatest battle would be the challenge of remaining faithful to God. Once his fighting days were over, he transitioned into a different role and became an

Teaching the Next Generation

effective executive leader. He successfully divided up the land among all the tribes. He established institutions like cities of refuge. And when he knew his life was almost over, it was time for his final expression of love as the leader of Israel. Joshua decided it was time for a speech.

This wasn't something he just rolled out of bed and did on a whim one day. Joshua knew it was one of his most important acts as the leader of God's people. The occasion of the speech was no small event, either. He had to plan the logistics of all the leaders of Israel—elders, heads, judges, and officers—gathering in one place. He had to write his speech, of course. Then, the day arrived for him to deliver his farewell address, as recounted in Joshua 23:1–5:

> *A long time afterward, when the LORD had given rest to Israel from all their surrounding enemies, and Joshua was old and well advanced in years, ² Joshua summoned all Israel, its elders and heads, its judges and leaders, and said to them, "I am now old and well advanced in years. ³ And you have seen all that the LORD your God has done to all these nations for your sake, for it is the LORD your God who has fought for you. ⁴ Behold, I have allotted to you as an inheritance for your tribes those nations that remain, along with all the nations that I have already cut off, from the Jordan to the Great Sea in the west. ⁵ The LORD your God will push them back before you and drive them out of your sight. And you shall possess their land, just as the LORD your God promised you.*

Joshua reminded them about all God had done, from Abraham all the way up to that very moment in the promised land. He recounted how God fought for Israel; every time a powerful enemy appeared, God drove them out just as he promised. Now Israel enjoyed peace on all sides.

Warnings from History

While the people had been set up for success, the future was still in question. Despite all God had done for them, Joshua had seen how they had a propensity to forget and drift away. Joshua saw it firsthand while Moses was still alive, when the people worshiped the golden calf in the wilderness. Joshua saw it when the Israelites fell in love with sexual idolatry at Peor and with the sin of Achan. In Joshua's last days, it was happening again—virtually every tribe failing to obey God's command and drive out the enemy. So, Joshua warned them about marrying outside God's people, having children with them, and compromising by worshiping their false gods. He relayed these warnings and instructions in Joshua 23:6–16:

> *Therefore, be very strong to keep and to do all that is written in the Book of the Law of Moses, turning aside from neither to the right hand nor to the left, ⁷ so that you may not mix with these nations remaining among you or make mention of the names of their gods or swear by them or serve them or bow down to them, ⁸ but you shall cling to the* LORD *your God just as you have done to this day. ⁹ For the* LORD *has driven out before you great and strong nations. And as for you, no man*

has been able to stand before you to this day. ¹⁰ One man of you puts to flight a thousand, since it is the LORD your God who fights for you, just as He promised you. ¹¹ Be very careful, therefore, to love the LORD your God. ¹² For if you turn back and cling to the remnant of these nations remaining among you and make marriages with them, so that you associate with them and they with you, ¹³ know for certain that the LORD your God will no longer drive out these nations before you, but they shall be a snare and a trap for you, a whip on your sides and thorns in your eyes, until you perish from off this good ground that the LORD your God has given you.

¹⁴ "And now I am about to go the way of all the earth [and die], and you know in your hearts and souls, all of you, that not one word has failed of all the good things that the LORD your God promised concerning you. All have come to pass for you; not one of them has failed. ¹⁵ But just as all the good things that the LORD your God promised concerning you have been fulfilled for you, so the LORD will bring upon you all the evil things, until he has destroyed you from off this good land that the LORD your God has given you, ¹⁶ if you transgress the covenant of the LORD your God, which he commanded you, and go and serve other gods and bow down to them. Then the anger of the LORD will be kindled against you, and you shall perish quickly from off the good land that he has given you."

Joshua warned the Israelites how the lifestyle of the Canaanites would draw them away and Israel could lose their inheritance. It was a sober, direct speech with both encouragement and warnings, from a man who loved God's people.

THEOLOGY—PASSING THE BATON

Encouragement and Warnings

Joshua was old and fully aware of his mortality, yet remained fully committed to God and concerned about the future for His people. He couldn't do everything he used to do, but he still had considerable wisdom and a history of loyalty to God. Joshua wanted desperately to encourage, prepare, and warn the next generation to be faithful to what God called them to do. He took this role just as seriously as he took the high-profile role of leading Israel across the Jordan into the land. He wanted to give clear warnings about the consequences of complacency and disobedience to God's commands.

Just as Joshua embraced the responsibility of preparing the next generation for success after he is gone, so did Paul. Like Joshua, Paul had a history of loyalty to God and was concerned Timothy and the churches would not stay faithful. So Paul wrote many letters to Timothy and the churches, some while suffering in prison and staring down a death sentence. Like Joshua's words to the Israelites, Paul's words in 1 Timothy 1:18–19 included both encouragement and warning:

> *This charge I entrust to you, Timothy, my child, in accordance with the prophecies previously made about you, [so] that by them you may wage the good warfare,*

> *¹⁹ holding faith and a good conscience. By rejecting this, some have made shipwreck of their faith . . .*

No Easy Task

Paul wanted to ensure Timothy and the churches were *never* ashamed of proclaiming the gospel to all the nations. He told them to cling closely to the sound doctrine and faith he had taught them, not waver to the left or right. No matter how hard it might get or how much the world might hate them, they must never give in to the pressure to compromise the truth. Like Joshua, Paul warned the churches about being sucked back into the wickedness of the people around them, as in 1 Timothy 6:9–10:

> *But those who desire to be rich fall into temptation, into a snare, into many senseless and harmful desires that plunge people into ruin and destruction. ¹⁰ For the love of money is a root of all kinds of evils. It is through this craving that some have wandered away from the faith and pierced themselves with many pangs.*

Paul warned them about the consequences of straying from faith and letting the world pull them away, but in 2 Timothy 3:12, he left no illusions that staying the course would be easy:

> *Indeed, all who desire to live a godly life in Christ Jesus will be persecuted.*

Following Jesus would be hard, and Paul didn't want the church to be surprised when they were scorned and ridiculed.

Just because you are following Jesus doesn't mean your life will feel "blessed" in earthly terms. In fact, it's often the opposite.

PERSONAL—TEACHING ONE ANOTHER

Generational and life experience barriers have no place among God's people. Our mission is far too important. I love how that younger generation of Israelites, out of respect, dropped what they were doing to come together to hear Joshua. Their lives were busy, no doubt, with kids, work, family, and household chores. There were lots of reasons not to go, but they showed up. In a similar way, Timothy took Paul's letters seriously. Most of the churches did, too. We can learn from this story of Joshua and the younger generation in Israel, from Paul, Timothy, and the churches. Can you see what Joshua did is what Jesus did for His disciples? How they passed it on and others to us today? We won't continue to draw more sojourners and seekers unless we invest in the ones we have already.

Both Paul and Joshua unified God's people. It's natural, even healthy, to form generational, demographic, or life experience subgroups in the church. But, we can't let our subgroups build barriers that keep us from living life together or compel us to compete for church resources. Jesus has not designed His church to live segmented, separated by these barriers. We need each other!

Being older, in the church, isn't only about age. It means those who've followed Jesus a long time, trained, discipled with a history of faithfulness. Like Israel in Joshua 23, we have many new believers who are hungry to learn! Like Joshua and Paul, we who've followed Jesus for a long time are commanded to encourage, teach, and prepare them for the calling God has given us. That's what Paul meant in 2 Timothy 2:2:

> ... and what you have heard from me in the presence of many witnesses entrust to faithful men, who will also be able [qualified] to teach others also.

So, we who are older must be intentional, doing what Paul instructed Timothy to do with new believers. It's on us to put in the work, like Joshua and Paul, to break down the barriers evil wants to build in the church. Just like old man Joshua and Paul in prison, we never quit Kingdom work, but our role within it does and should change. God wants us who are advanced in years to love, mentor, equip, encourage, and teach our younger family.

Being younger isn't only about age, either, among God's people. It also indicates those who are brand new to following Jesus. We older (more experienced) members of the church come alongside them and love them! And younger followers of Jesus, listen, it's not just on us elders to find you and teach. You have an undeniable job, too, summarized in Hebrews 13:7:

> Remember your leaders, those who spoke to you the word of God. Consider the outcome of their way of life, and imitate their faith.

Hebrews 13:17 elaborates on this instruction:

Obey your leaders and submit to them, for they are keeping watch over your souls, as those who will have to give an account. Let them do this with joy and not with groaning, for that would be of no advantage to you.

Like Timothy and the younger Israelites, you must make it a priority to seek, connect, and learn from older followers of Jesus. We have seen God do many things you have not. We've experienced God's faithfulness, seen Him keep His promises. We have been through tragedy, and we've made many mistakes. We know firsthand the consequences of unfaithfulness. We aren't better or smarter than you young Jesus-followers; we've just already made the errors many of you are thinking about making right now! Walk in unity with us. Learn from us.

But, make it as easy as you can, and joyful, for the older among us to do our job. Be available; be teachable; listen to your elders when they try to teach you about the goodness and mercy of our Jesus. Be hungry for the wisdom you can glean from our experiences, our failures, and our stories about God's faithfulness. Heed our warnings about the consequences of wandering from our Jesus, about what unfaithfulness can cost you.

Followers of Jesus, don't hang out only with people your age or people just like you. Don't live behind barriers with other young people or other old people, other people with families, or other people in recovery. Don't just seek ways to only be with people like you. Come together in the love of

Jesus, unified in the Great Commission to go forth, baptize, and teach all He has commanded. Older saints, it's on us to build relationships with younger saints in the church family and teach them all we have learned. Younger saints, it's on you to seek out relationships with us elders and learn everything you can while you can.

When the older followers do as Joshua did and the younger followers are like Timothy, it builds powerful unity, which evil hates. It will make our mission as Jesus' church more beautiful and successful. It will also ensure our next generation is trained, equipped, and ready to be faithful to continue going into the land when the rest of us are gone. We must overcome any barriers between us by teaching one another so we can continue going into the land with the gospel.

CHAPTER TWENTY-THREE

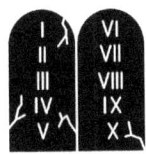

A Monument for Renewal
(Joshua 24:1–28)

Have you ever missed an exit on a familiar route? Maybe you were driving to a regular destination, got distracted, and missed the turn? Without GPS and the annoying voice reminding you to turn in two hundred feet, it's easy to miss the signs. Once, I was driving home and blew past my exit by ten miles! Why did I do that? I wasn't paying attention, talking on the phone, and missed all the signs. Before I knew it, I had flown right past my exit. I yelled out words of "righteous thanksgiving and praise" when I realized my mistake. We've all done something like that—missed an exit or made a wrong turn on a familiar route. It's part of being human.

Has this ever happened to you as a follower of Jesus? You genuinely want to follow Him, but something distracts, wounds, tempts, or lures you away. The fact is, even though Jesus has done so much for us and promises to do more, we are prone to wander. Just when you think you have following Jesus figured out, you miss an exit or take a wrong turn. Suddenly, you realize you've gotten off the righteous path and ask yourself, "How did I get here?" The truth is, we regularly need monuments or markers to remind us of the path we need to keep.

History—Israel Wasn't Listening

Cycles of Forgetfulness

Some time after Joshua's farewell address, it seems the Israelites were still wandering from what he had taught them. So, Joshua gathered everyone once again, this time at Shechem, where Abraham built his first altar to God (see Genesis 12). This was the place where God first made His covenant with Abraham, making it special.

This time, Joshua's message was directly from God. God spoke through Joshua, reminding them of His faithfulness to them: He recounted His grace for Abraham, Isaac, Jacob, Esau, Moses, and Aaron in Egypt, the crossing of the Red Sea, His defeat of the Amorite kings, the story of Balaam, the wilderness journey, and the Israelites' entry into the promised land. God reminded them He gave them land they didn't earn, cities they didn't build, and vineyards they did not plant. He had done everything He promised and more! Yet, Israel still forgot, wandered, and failed to follow with faithful hearts. Despite God's warnings about the dangers of Canaanite influences, they didn't remember or didn't listen. They continued making the same mistakes, worshiping gods of nations God had defeated for them! Some even returned to worshiping the gods of the golden calf their grandparents created in the wilderness.

Why would Israel wander so easily and be so foolish to worship the gods of defeated nations? After all God had done, how could they take this wrong turn toward the immoral lifestyle of the Canaanites? They needed to get back on track and start fresh.

Joshua Builds a Monument

Joshua gave the Israelites a choice. In Joshua 24:14–15, he drew a clear line in the sand, something many are afraid to do today when it comes to the gospel:

> *Now therefore fear the* LORD *and serve him in sincerity and in faithfulness. Put away [get rid of] the gods that your fathers served beyond the River and in Egypt, and serve the* LORD. *[15] And if it is evil in your eyes to serve the* LORD, *choose this day whom you will serve, whether the gods your fathers served in the region beyond the River, or the gods of the Amorites in whose land you dwell. But as for me and my house, we will serve the* LORD.

"Israel," he said in effect, "you say you want to serve God, but you can't. You're distracted by these other gods and you take the wrong exit. Choose who you will serve! If you don't want to serve God, then pick your favorite false god and go for it. You do you! If you really want to serve God, you will need to get rid of all your fake idols and drive those people out of the land. But, as for my household and family, we will serve God."

There was no halfway; they were either all in or all out. It turned out, the Israelites wanted to be faithful, as recounted in Joshua 24:16–24:

> Then the people answered, "Far be it from us that we should forsake the LORD to serve other gods, [17] for it is the LORD our God who brought us and our fathers up from the land of Egypt, out of the house of slavery, and who did those great signs in our sight and preserved us in all the way that we went, and among all the peoples through whom we passed. [18] And the LORD drove out before us all the peoples, the Amorites who lived in the land. Therefore we also will serve the LORD, for he is our God."
>
> [19] But Joshua said to the people, "You are not able to serve the LORD, for he is a holy God. He is a jealous God; he will not forgive your transgressions or your sins. [20] If you forsake the LORD and serve foreign gods, then he will turn and do you harm and consume you, after having done you good." [21] And the people said to Joshua, "No, but we will serve the LORD." [22] Then Joshua said to the people, "You are witnesses against yourselves that you have chosen the LORD, to serve him." And they said, "We are witnesses." [23] He said, "Then put away the foreign gods that are among you,

and incline your heart to the LORD, the God of Israel."
²⁴ And the people said to Joshua, "The LORD our God we will serve, and his voice we will obey."

Israel decided to get back on track and choose to serve the Lord—and they really meant it this time! They and Joshua, together in community, made a new covenant, and Joshua retaught them what obedience would look like. Then, Joshua built a huge stone monument at Shechem with God's instructions and promises engraved on it, described in Joshua 24:25–28:

> *So Joshua made a covenant with the people that day, and put in place statutes and rules for them at Shechem. ²⁶ And Joshua wrote these words in the Book of the Law of God. And he took a large stone and set it under the terebinth that was by the sanctuary of the LORD. ²⁷ And Joshua said to all the people, "Behold, this stone shall be a witness against us, for it has heard all the words of the LORD that he spoke to us. Therefore it shall be a witness against you, lest you deal falsely with your God." ²⁸ So Joshua sent the people away, every man to his inheritance.*

THEOLOGY—A CYCLE OF WANDERING

Israel's history was filled with these frustrating cycles of repeatedly committing, forgetting, wandering, and returning. When they did come back, it was usually with a national gathering; repentance took place, and monuments were built. Such events took place at Mount Sinai (Exodus 19–

24), Moab (Deuteronomy 29–30), Gilgal (Joshua 5:2–9), the first Passover in the promised land (Joshua 5:10–12), Mount Ebal (Joshua 8:30–35), and Shechem (Joshua 24), and under King Asa (2 Chronicles 15), King Jehoiada (2 Kings 11:17), King Hezekiah (2 Chronicles 29–31), King Josiah (2 Kings 23 and 2 Chronicles 34), and Nehemiah and Ezra (Nehemiah 8–10). That's a lot of monuments to restoration, right? Well, that's not even all of them, only the major ones. The Israelites would make these promises to God, break them, repent, recommit, and then wander, repeating the cycle.

After all God had done, was doing, and continued to do for them, why couldn't Israel just be faithful—like we (think we) are? Their perpetual cycle of wandering reveals how God's people need continual reminders about His goodness. You'd think this would be frustrating to God, but it doesn't surprise Him when we constantly wander. In fact, every time His children stray, nothing thrills the Father more than when we come home!

When Israel wandered, there was a long list of laws and ceremonies to perform for restoration, but not for us. This is the beauty of the new covenant God has made with us through the work of Jesus on the cross. What Jesus did on the cross created a far superior restoration process than what our Old Testament brothers and sisters had. Jesus did away with temple sacrifices, stone monuments, and reliance on a priesthood. He wiped all of that out at the cross. Remember when Jesus told the story of the prodigal son and compared the joy of his father with the joy of our Father in heaven, in Luke 15:7:

Just so, I tell you, there will be more joy in heaven over one sinner who repents than over ninety-nine righteous persons who need no repentance.

Our heavenly Father loves it so much when wanderers return home to Him, He makes the map simple to read, as expressed in 1 John 1:9:

If we confess our sins, he is faithful and just to forgive us our sins and to cleanse us from all unrighteousness.

Through the cross, Jesus has made His chosen people righteous even though we are still prone to wander. When we do wander, instead of old man Joshua, it's the Spirit who calls us, reminding us that we now belong to Him. The Spirit reveals where we went wrong, reminds us of what Jesus has done, and guides His chosen back to the flock. The Spirit gives us the gift of sorrow over our sin, the obedience of confession, and a supernatural desire for repentance. So, while our pattern of wandering is the same as Israel, our path to restoration is far superior through Jesus!

PERSONAL—JESUS BUILDS A MONUMENT

Jesus knew we would need a monument to remember how to get home when we wander. In Chapter Six, we saw how the Israelites loved building monuments to their moments of restoration, as a way to keep themselves mindful of the need for faithfulness. We, the church, also need a monument to God's faithfulness and restoration with the Father. Jesus built us that monument.

Do you remember how somber Jesus was when He was celebrating Passover with His disciples the night before He was to die? It wasn't just because of the brutal death He was about to face. He also carried a heavy burden for what those closest to Him were about to endure—the failures they would experience. Judas was about to give in to the evil one and exchange loyalty to Jesus for money. Peter, who Jesus said would be the rock of His church, would deny three times he even knew who Jesus was, out of fear! Jesus had warned Peter how Satan would seek to destroy him, but Peter forgot that warning.

What about the rest of the disciples? Many times, Jesus told them He would die and conquer death in three days. The disciples witnessed Jesus do miraculous things, proving He was God and that His promises could be trusted. When the time came, they failed to trust what He said despite witnessing His power over and over again. Like Israel, they wandered, ran in fear, and were ready to abandon both the Lord and their calling in the kingdom of God. In fact, they were ready to just return to their old jobs, their old pointless empty lives from before they met Jesus. Just like the Israelites, and just like us, they failed, faltered, and scattered in compromise, fear, and self-preservation.

Their collective abandonment and betrayal are emblematic of our same propensity to forsake divine love. Our Jesus knew His apostles would need a powerful monument to remind them and help them find their way back. Jesus knew we, His church, would need to recommit ourselves constantly. He knew following Him would be hard, and evil would encourage us in our natural tendency to wander unfaithfully, so He built a monument way better than any stone memorial. His people could rebuild this monument anywhere they gathered.

In fact, building this monument, the Lord's table, became one of the commands Jesus told His apostles to "teach all nations" to observe. They were to teach the church that each time they gathered and built this monument, they were to remember what Jesus had done for them. The apostles faithfully taught the church how to build this monument, which has become our monument, too!

Unlike the monument of Joshua and the Israelites, the Lord's table is not a monument about us keeping our promises; it's about Jesus keeping His. It's a monument to what Jesus promised—how at the cross He died for us and conquered death when He rose again. This monument reminds us that our standing with God isn't based on our strength but on Christ's finished work on the cross. Because as much as we want to follow the Lamb wherever He goes, we are so weak! We are prone to wander, miss our exit, and need to find our way back. Many idols cause us to wander, demanding our allegiance and making us forget what Jesus has done for us. Money, immorality, resentment, revenge for people who hurt us, relationships—it's a miracle we can be faithful at all! It's good to be reminded on a regular basis how easy it is for us to lose our way, because we will forget.

Are you like Israel? Are there temptations in your life causing you to forget the goodness of God's grace? That's why we, too, need a monument to God's grace, reminding us we ourselves aren't the ones keeping us faithful. Jesus is.

Just as there were serious warnings written on Joshua's monument, our monument comes with cautions, too, which Paul noted in 1 Corinthians 11:27–29:

> *Whoever, therefore, eats the bread or drinks the cup of the Lord in an unworthy manner will be guilty concerning the body and blood of the Lord. *^{28}* Let a person examine himself, then, and so eat of the bread and drink of the cup. *^{29}* For anyone who eats and drinks without discerning the body eats and drinks judgment on himself.*

His words warn us to remember what this monument is about. Our righteousness, our confession, and our repentance are not our own. Followers of Jesus are completely reliant on what Jesus has done for us. The Lord's table is about remembering we are prone to wander and about having the humility to be reconciled to God and one another. Some people think they don't need to be reminded, because they believe they've come to a place in life where they don't really sin much anymore. Like resentment, that arrogance has no place at the Lord's table. Anyone who comes to this monument without complete, humble reliance upon the gospel and the cross isn't welcome.

Follower of Jesus, do you want to come home? Do you want forgiveness, righteousness, and restoration? Are you joyfully fully reliant upon what Jesus has done for you? Then remember, you are welcome when His followers gather to build a precious monument at His table. He makes it all possible.

Go into the Land!

CHAPTER TWENTY-FOUR

A Legacy Inspiring Faithfulness
(Joshua 24:29–33)

It's remarkable how the stories of Joshua and the Israelites come alive in Scripture, connecting us to their legacies in the story of redemption. The parallels between God's commands to Joshua and Jesus' commands to us are profound. Joshua led God's people into the land without hesitation, in unified obedience. Jesus has commanded His church to go into all nations likewise, with resolve and common purpose. As God promised Joshua His abiding presence, Jesus promised, "I am with you always, to the end of the age" (Matthew 28:20). And just as Joshua led Israel into enemy strongholds to claim God's promised inheritance, we are sent into enemy strongholds to proclaim the victory of Christ's eternal kingdom.

The conclusion of Joshua's story, including the first verse of the following book, challenges us to consider what kind of legacy we're leaving behind. Have we truly absorbed the lessons God taught the Israelites in their conquest of Canaan? To build a legacy faithful to the mission Jesus gave us, we have to let these truths transform us as individuals and as church communities.

HISTORY—A LEGACY OF FAITHFULNESS

A Conqueror and a Prophet

After a remarkable life, Joshua died. He was a faithful follower of God and a loyal, talented leader for seventy years. He led Israel in the conquest of Canaan and created governing structures, like the cities of refuge, as the tribes settled in their new home. Joshua also led Israel in powerful moments of corporate worship that drew in outsiders to become worshipers of God, like the sojourners at Mount Ebal.

Joshua led as a prophet—speaking for God, inspiring the people when they were afraid, and affirming them when they were obedient. Several times, when Israel wandered from God, Joshua admonished them and shepherded them back to faithfulness. As much as Israel mourned Moses' death, the loss of Joshua was even harder. He was the last of that generation that crossed both the Red Sea and the Jordan River into Canaan.

The account of Joshua's death and burial is found in Joshua 24:29–33:

After these things Joshua the son of Nun, the servant of the LORD, *died, being 110 years old.* ³⁰ *And they buried him in his own inheritance at Timnath-serah, which is in the hill country of Ephraim, north of the mountain of Gaash.*

³¹ *Israel served the* LORD *all the days of Joshua, and all the days of the elders who outlived Joshua and had known all the work that the* LORD *did for Israel.*

³² *As for the bones of Joseph, which the people of Israel brought up from Egypt, they buried them at Shechem, in the piece of land that Jacob bought from the sons of Hamor the father of Shechem for a hundred pieces of money. It became an inheritance of the descendants of Joseph.*

³³ *And Eleazar the son of Aaron died, and they buried him at Gibeah, the town of Phinehas his son, which had been given him in the hill country of Ephraim.*

A New Generation

All these revered patriarchs were buried in places given to them as inheritances by God, a beautiful way to honor them. The deaths and burials of Joshua and Eleazar, and the reburial of Joseph, who by faith asked for his bones to be taken from Egypt to his homeland, marked a transition to the next generation. Joshua's death marked the end of an era, yet Israel still had work to do.

That younger generation of Israelites honored Joshua not only by burying him in his yard but also by following his example. They continued to serve God faithfully after Joshua had departed from their lives. And they knew they needed to finish going in and taking the land, as revealed in the epilogue to the book of Joshua, found in Judges 1:1:

> After the death of Joshua, the people of Israel inquired of the LORD, "Who shall go up first for us against the Canaanites, to fight against them?"

Israel had to finish their conquest of Canaan without Joshua, but they recalled lessons learned from the past. Remember how Israel was deceived by the Gibeonites because they failed to inquire of the Lord? Even under Joshua, Israel had forgotten the importance of relying upon the presence of God every step of the way. They remembered that lesson now and handled this new challenge exactly how Joshua would have handled it.

This is why the end of the book of Joshua notes the death of Eleazar, the priest who inquired of the Lord for Joshua. His son Phinehas, the new high priest, now took on that role, asking God, "How should we continue the conquest? Who should do it?"

THEOLOGY—WALKING IN THEIR FOOTSTEPS

Let's go back to where Joshua's legacy began. When Moses died, God gave Joshua a very important commission, encapsulated in Joshua 1:2–9:

A Legacy Inspiring Faithfulness

Now therefore arise, go over this Jordan, you and all this people, into the land that I am giving to them, to the people of Israel.... ⁵... I will not leave you or forsake you. ⁶ Be strong and courageous, for you shall cause this people to inherit the land that I swore to their fathers to give them. ⁷ Only be strong and very courageous, being careful to do according to all the law that Moses my servant commanded you. Do not turn from it to the right hand or to the left, [so] that you may have good success wherever you go.... ⁹ Have I not commanded you? Be strong and courageous. Do not be frightened, and do not be dismayed, for the LORD your God is with you wherever you go.

God gave Joshua his commission and a promise: "Go into the land and do everything I have commanded you to do." But it wasn't going to be easy. Joshua would need to be strong and courageous every step of the way. Every nation in Canaan would hate them for what God had called them to do, but Joshua was to be courageous because God promised never to leave him or forget about Him, even on the days when he failed or missed an exit.

Joshua wasn't perfect, but he was faithful. He obeyed God to the best of his abilities. Because of his legacy, the next generation had an example to learn from and follow. Role models for faithful living are so important! In Hebrews 11, there is a list of people with a similar legacy, who inspired faithfulness in others who came after them. The person listed in Hebrews 11:30–31 is someone we learned about in the story of Joshua:

> *By faith, the walls of Jericho fell down after they had been encircled for seven days.* ³¹ *By faith, Rahab the prostitute did not perish with those who were disobedient because she gave a friendly welcome to the spies.*

As great a legacy as Joshua left, he isn't listed in Hebrews 11, but Rahab, the prostitute who helped the Israelite scouts at Jericho, is. Rahab was a Gentile woman whom God's grace transformed into a timeless example of faithfulness and the power of redemption. She became an inspiration to every outsider who found their way to that great worship service at Mount Ebal. Like Joshua, she wasn't perfect, but she was faithful.

Rahab's legacy as an outsider transformed by grace is perhaps more inspiring for us than Joshua's. Many of you know how it feels to be on the outside and then, by grace, be brought into the family of God. As you worship Jesus and go into the land with His gospel, can you relate to Rahab's legacy—her story of God's grace? Rahab is part of what the writer of Hebrews called a cloud of witnesses in Hebrews 12:1–2, inspiring us to stay faithful and never give up:

> *Therefore, since we are surrounded by so great a cloud of witnesses, let us also lay aside every weight and sin which clings so closely, and let us run with endurance the race that is set before us,* ² *looking to Jesus, the founder and perfecter of our faith, who for the joy that was set before him endured the cross, despising the shame, and is seated at the right hand of the throne of God.*

The cloud of witnesses God was building didn't stop there. He continued building it when He sent the Holy Spirit. The apostles became part of that cloud once they found their way back to Jesus after the resurrection. Through God's grace, they became examples of courage and faithfulness, teaching us how to remain faithful. And we need their legacy for the commission Jesus has given us to go into the land and take it with the gospel.

PERSONAL—OUR LEGACY OF REDEMPTION

Whose legacy inspires you to be faithful to Jesus? Will your legacy as a Jesus follower, in carrying out the Great Commission, inspire others the same way? We have established throughout this book how similar Joshua's commission is to the one Jesus gave us in Matthew 28:19–20:

> *Go therefore and make disciples of all nations, baptizing them in the name of the Father and of the Son and of the Holy Spirit, [20] teaching them to observe all that I have commanded you. And behold, I am with you always, to the end of the age.*

But, this commission Jesus gave to the apostles, passed through generations to us today, is much harder than Joshua's. Our inheritance isn't just Canaan; it's the entire world. We have been called to go take it with the gospel. Our calling to go to all nations with a gospel evil despises more than it despised Joshua or the Israelites. That's why Jesus said to be surprised when the world hates you because of His commands. Yet, He also made a promise. Just as He did for Joshua, He promises He'll never leave us or forget about us as we do what He's commanded.

Meanwhile, the cloud of witnesses inspiring our faithfulness continues to grow and will continue until Jesus returns. It's a bigger cloud of witnesses than Joshua had or the apostles had. It's bigger today than at any time in church history. The cloud of witnesses around us is filled with miraculous stories of each one of God's redeemed, including yours.

Do you think Israel had lots of stories about God's power? Do you think Jericho and Rahab were inspirational stories? The church has seen much bigger walls come tumbling down for the sake of the gospel than the ones at Jericho. The church is filled with stories of outsiders brought into God's family through the cross, the good news of Jesus' death and resurrection. Our stories are even more miraculous and inspirational than God parting a river or defeating Canaanite kings. The miracles of transformation God works in our lives add to the massive cloud of witnesses surrounding us. Let's face it, these witnesses are a lot better than burial sites. Our legacy is full of Jerichos and Rahabs! This cloud of witnesses, along with the Holy Spirit and the power of the gospel, keeps us faithful as we go into the land.

There are people in this cloud of witnesses who fill my heart with tremendous love and affection when I remember them. My first pastor, Al Cockrell; my first professor, Norman Spotts; my beloved mentors, Tom Fillinger and Coach Bowden. I'm part of the legacy of this cloud of witnesses who

A Legacy Inspiring Faithfulness

have passed on. Their stories and their lessons surround me, each a significant part of who I am as a follower of Jesus.

The members of my church family, inspiring me to keep going in faith, are part of the legacy of this cloud of witnesses, too. When I'm tempted to wander, forget, or get complacent, they are like the Israelites' stone-pile monuments, reminding me of God's commands and His provision. God teaches me through their faithful words and actions—not just in their successes, but also in the way they've handled their failures, and the mercy with which they've handled mine. I'm grateful for all I've learned from their stories of how God is using them to refine one another and expand His kingdom.

Do you see how God can use a cloud of witnesses to inspire you to follow the Lamb? Consider whose legacies in this cloud of witnesses inspire your personal faithfulness to what God has called you to do. You could list several right now in your head, some still alive and some who have died. There is no greater way to honor their legacy than to follow in their footsteps as we go into the land together. Stories like Joshua, Rahab, and ours remind us Jesus will keep His promise: He'll never leave us or forget about us. Be faithful as they were or are, right now alongside you, as Jesus brings new outsiders to join us.

There is another side to this lesson. As you go into the land, God is making you part of the cloud of witnesses, too. You have a responsibility to the community of the faithful not to be selfish with your precious redemption story. Be a witness! God's people need your legacy.

Does that make you nervous? Do you think your legacy could never inspire others to be strong, courageous, and faithful? Here's what I can say: if God's grace kept Joshua faithful, transformed Rahab into an inspiration, and brought the apostles back from such colossal failure to become faithful, He will do the same for you if you have the gift of faith. You don't have to be Joshua to be part of this cloud; you just must be redeemed. Then, our Jesus will do the rest. Faith that doesn't leave a legacy, the book of James tells us, isn't really faith at all.

To be blessed by this cloud of witnesses, and to be part of this cloud, you must be around it. Do you desire to do all the Lord commands, to be "strong and courageous" like Joshua, Rahab, and others before you were? The first step is gathering often with the cloud of witnesses Jesus is assembling. Without them, you'll never build a legacy of being strong and courageous. You'll never have what it takes to go into the land and do all our Jesus has commanded. You'll never experience the joy of His promise never to leave you or forsake you. Because among the cloud of witnesses is where that promise, from our Jesus to us, is kept.

As we conclude this book, let's remember the beautiful correlations between God's command to Joshua and Jesus' command to us. Just as Joshua was called to lead Israel into the promised land, we are called to take the gospel to all nations. This mission is challenging, but we are empowered by the promise that Jesus will be with us always. The cloud of witnesses—those faithful followers of Jesus before us and among us—reminds us of God's faithfulness and inspires us to persevere. Let us go into the land with courage, faithfulness, and the assurance that our legacy of redemption will inspire future generations, from now to the Day of the Lord.

Go into the Land!

About the Author

Joe is the founding pastor of GraceLife Church in Sarasota, Florida (www.gracelifesrq.com). He holds doctorates in divinity and theology, a master's degree in theology, a bachelor's degree in biblical studies, and another in pastoral studies.

After beginning vocational ministry at age eighteen, Joe spent his first twenty-two years of ministry as a youth pastor and an outreach pastor in three different churches. He coached high school football and basketball for nearly twenty years.

In 2008, Joe founded Mobilepreacher.org (www.mobilepreacher.org), an organization designed to help seasoned ministers create ministries that might not fit inside traditional church walls. He is also the founder and executive director of the Nightlife Center in Sarasota (www.nightlifecenter.org).

Joe is husband to Laura and father to Ben. You can find him on X (@mobilepreacher), Instagram (@Mobilepreacher), and Facebook (facebook.com/JosephDavisBooks).

MORE BOOKS BY DR. JOSEPH DAVIS

Letters from Heaven:
A Devotional Guide Through Revelation

The Grace Life: What Philippians Teaches Us About Loving One Another Relentlessly

Surviving in Egypt: The Life of Joseph

Swimming Lessons: The Story of Jonah

Growing to Love God's Word:
An In-Depth Study of Psalm 119

Scan the code below to follow Joe on Facebook!

And a quick request . . .

While *Go into the Land!* is still fresh in your mind and heart, please take a few minutes to leave an honest review on Amazon.

Your feedback helps readers who might enjoy and be blessed by this study of Joshua to find it and Joe's other books.

Thank you!

www.ingramcontent.com/pod-product-compliance
Lightning Source LLC
Chambersburg PA
CBHW070838160426
43192CB00012B/2228